When Fragments Make a Whole

When Fragments Make a Whole

*A Personal Journey Through
Healing Stories in the Bible*

Lory Widmer Hess

Publisher's note
This book is based on the experiences and recollections of the author. In some cases, names of people and places have been changed to protect privacy.

Scripture quotations are from The ESV® Bible
(The Holy Bible, English Standard Version®) © 2001 by Crossway, a publishing ministry of Good News Publishers
Used by permission. All rights reserved.

First published by Floris Books in 2024
© 2024 Lory Widmer Hess

Lory Widmer Hess has asserted her right under the Copyright, Design and Patents Act 1988
to be identified as the Author of this Work
All rights reserved. No part of this book may be reproduced in any form without written permission of Floris Books, Edinburgh
www.florisbooks.co.uk

 Also available as an eBook

British Library CIP Data available
ISBN 978-178250-895-3

Contents

Preface	7
Introduction	12
1. A Man with an Unclean Spirit	22
2. A Woman with a Fever	35
3. A Leper	46
4. An Invalid by the Pool of Bethesda	58
5. A Man with a Withered Hand	71
6. A Centurion's Servant	82
7. The Young Man of Nain	96
8. A Demon-possessed Man in the Tombs	108
9. A Bleeding Woman and a Dying Girl	120
10. A Gentile Woman's Daughter	131
11. A Deaf Man	146
12. A Blind Man	158
13. A Boy with Seizures	173
14. A Woman with a Disabling Spirit	191
15. A Man with Dropsy	201
16. Ten Lepers	212
17. A Blind Man of Jericho	222
18. Lazarus	236
Afterword	251
Appendix 1: The Anthroposophical View of Christ and Human Evolution	256
Appendix 2: The Healing Stories in the Synoptic Gospels	261
Notes	264
Bibliography	271

Break a vase, and the love that reassembles the fragments is stronger than that love which took its symmetry for granted when it was whole.

Derek Walcott, Nobel Prize Lecture, 1992

Preface

What gives me the authority to write a book about healing, and healing in the gospels at that? I am not a doctor or a nurse, a therapist or a counselor. Nor am I a pastor, a priest, a theologian, a Biblical scholar or a historian. How could I have the temerity to imagine that my thoughts about the healing process might be of help or of interest to anyone else?

I may not have any official credentials or stamp of approval upon my knowledge of healing, but I do have the experience of being someone who has been healed through relationship with Christ, and through a deepened connection with the human community toward which Christ seeks to guide us. My condition lasted for many years and touched me on many levels: body, soul and spirit. It kept me from being able to speak or even to cognize my own deepest truth. It caused me to hurt people, to bungle relationships, to add chaos and disorder to a world already suffering far too much from dysfunctional human activity.

However, this condition did not prevent me from maintaining the appearance of normality, as I went to school, to work, and even raised a family. It was seldom apparent to anyone else in its full extent. Most people only noticed one aspect of it if they noticed anything at all. Even my closest loved ones and colleagues were largely blind to what was going on inside me. And so, even though for a long time I felt unable to live a full or satisfying life, I was never completely pulled out of life, either. I didn't have to be hospitalized or spend time in a psychiatric clinic. I was not labelled with an official diagnosis or put on drugs. Much of my suffering took place in silence, behind a mask. Only toward the end of the process did I gain the courage to admit that I needed time and support in order to heal and to speak about my experiences.

Because of this, I know there must be other people who are also suffering in this way, who maintain a seemingly 'normal' outer life while inwardly they feel themselves to be paralyzed or dying. I am daring to write this book for them, to tell them that they are not alone and that there is hope. If you can identify what you need and dare to reach out for it, then the Healer will meet you there in that place of courageous self-knowledge. I know this from my own experience, and I also know that this healing is available to everyone, not just me, or it would not be true healing. Out of the depths of what I have endured, I want to pass on a message that may give strength to others who are similarly struggling.

Although not a healing professional, I am a reader, a writer, and a lifelong student of language and literature. I've worked as an editor and graphic designer, striving to craft words and images in a way that is meaningful, inspiring and true. Language has been the great love of my life, even at the times when it seemed to become the greatest stumbling block. Insofar as the gospels are stories, crafted in artistic language, I therefore have some experience in how to navigate them. Long before I started to study the Bible or to cultivate a conscious relationship with Christ, I was steeped in the magic of story, finding in it my own personal savior. How this personal salvation eventually became connected with the Savior of the world, and how my love of story eventually guided me to recognize and claim my own healing story, forms much of the background of this book. If you, too, love language and find relief for your suffering through narrative, I hope it will resonate with you.

Along the way I earned a diploma from the School of Eurythmy in Spring Valley, New York. Eurythmy is a performance art arising out of anthroposophy, the spiritual world view and path of knowledge described by the Austrian philosopher Rudolf Steiner (1861–1925). Described as 'visible speech' and 'visible singing', eurythmy also has applications in education and medical therapy. It aims to make the whole human being the visible expression of what otherwise happens invisibly in the soul when we speak or make music. As you can imagine, participating in eurythmy training is not a straightforward matter for a secretly ill person; nevertheless, eurythmy played a significant role in my healing journey.

In the course of that journey, I found and joined the Christian Community, a sister movement to anthroposophy that is inspired by its insights but whose main function is to be a renewal of the ritual stream of Christian worship. Through the creation of communities that celebrate the sacraments in a form appropriate to modern consciousness, it is a vessel for the working of Christ in human bodies and souls. This, too, has been a major factor in my own story.

My most important learning experiences, though, were ones that carried no degree, certificate, membership or outer recognition whatsoever. My instructors were people who had no power or authority in this world, no voice and no ability to speak up for themselves, but everything to teach me about the most important things in life and its true foundation in the sacrificial power of love. Those teachers were firstly my son, Brendan, who came to me at the time of my greatest need as a messenger from the world of the angels, and secondly those developmentally disabled individuals I have worked with in communities in the United States and Switzerland, who had the patience to continue teaching me when I had a hard time comprehending my son's message. My debt to them is immeasurable and cannot be expressed in words, although I will try.

I have also learned so much from my co-sufferer and companion in the journey of life, my husband, Michael Widmer. Our marriage has been a crucible and a catalyst for healing, and I could not have come to this point without it. I thank him, as well as our son, for allowing me to describe some of our adventures together, and for continuing to be my greatest support and comfort as we continue on our way.

All of these people and many others were part of my story, helping to pull me back from the brink of death and into life and community. I cannot describe all of them in the course of this book, but to them go my profound thanks.

However qualified or otherwise I may be to write a book like this, I take comfort in knowing that the gospels were not written to be the province of scholars or academics or experts of any kind. They were created as a training manual for people in need of healing, people challenged to take up the task of evolving the new kind of faith that would make them whole. No one is either too humble or too grand for that calling, and no expertise is required other than a willingness to honestly ask what it means to be human. In that, we are all equal.

This book is a work of imaginative devotion rather than a product of scholarship, and incorporates facts and observations that have been interesting and helpful to me. The stories drawn from my personal life are included as my testimony to the power of the Healing Spirit, which I can only offer from my own point of view. I am convinced that this healing activity, or at least its potential, can be found in anyone's life if one looks in the right way. Any responses to this work, or any communications about how readers have worked in similar or different ways on this content, would be gratefully received.

Thank you for joining me in this sacred reading space, and for being a witness of and a participant in the great story that includes us all. I wish for you the blessings of peace and joyful expectation that are offered to us by the Healing Spirit, our comforter and advocate, who accompanies each one of us when things seem most dark and hopeless. At those times, let us remember the words of Jacques Lusseyran: 'Light is in us, even when we have no eyes.'[1]

Introduction

Many people devote all their efforts to preserving and securing their existence in the material world. Even religious or spiritual efforts may be devoted to this end, whether the aim is security and prosperity now, or in the next world, which is conceived of as a copy or a continuation of this one.

In his book *Falling Upward*, the Franciscan priest Richard Rohr calls these the concerns of the 'first half' of life. It's legitimate for a young person to build a 'container' in which to dwell, along with a firm sense of their identity and their place in the world. But at some point, we each need to consider what the container is actually meant to hold, even giving it over in service to the whole rather than keeping it for the benefit of our own personal existence. Otherwise we miss the chance to enter the 'second half' of life, and this 'half' is not necessarily a temporal measurement but indicates a shift in focus.[1]

If one only considers the security and integrity of the container, then illness is a threat and death is THE END. Both are to be struggled with and overcome, or avoided and denied at all costs. That is the attitude taken by our outer, materialistically focused culture.

But if our lives are solely dedicated to building and maintaining our container, it becomes a prison. Often our one-sided preoccupation with what is only meant to be a single step on the path toward true life must be transformed through some kind of disruption: illness, loss, divorce, failure, death. What seemed like a threat and obstacle can then become a doorway through which one reaches another, higher level of existence, a level that transcends but also embraces the first. Symptoms may turn out to be messengers, catalysts for needed change. Through patterns of generational trauma and communal healing we might find out how we are connected to others. Intractable physical challenges may push us to cultivate inner capacities. We may move from merely persisting in our 'survival dance' to joining the 'sacred dance', as Rohr puts it.

Sadly, many people never progress to this stage. Fear of illness and death, along with resistance to much-needed change, present the greatest obstacle to making the transition. We have to find a way not to fight against these realities, but to comprehend and move through them on our way to a wider existence.

At the beginning of the gospel narratives of Christ's ministry, we are called by John the Baptist to repent.[2] But the word usually translated as 'repentance', *metanoia*, is better understood as indicating a complete change of heart and mind. The way of Christ involves a turning upside down and inside out of the values and methods of the first half of life. It doesn't deny or oppose them in their own realm, but brings them to the next level so that we won't fall prey to death through remaining stuck to our container.

In line with this picture, one of Rudolf Steiner's most revelatory insights was that the sensory world and the thinking connected with it were created not as a permanent home for humanity, but to form the basis for freedom. However, we need the impulse of spiritual activity that surges up within this sensory container, transforming it and bringing it forward, if we are to go beyond the first step on that journey. In freedom, we have the potential to perform *metanoia* and cross over into a new phase of evolution, to become a new order of being in the universe. At the Incarnation this happened on the macrocosmic level when the deed of Christ provided the impulse for the whole earth to cross over into the second half of evolution. With this as a model, the same thing has to happen within the microcosm of each individual life. Two thousand years later, however, we are still struggling to catch up.

The Children's Service of the Christian Community, which is a remarkable storehouse of pithy wisdom, describes Christ as the one 'who leads what is living into death that it may live anew; who leads what is dead into life that it may behold the spirit'. The goal is not eternal life in the material world, but participation in the eternal cycle of living. We bring to it, as our special contribution to the whole, our enduring, evolving human consciousness.

The stories of Christ's healings in the gospels, therefore, cannot be understood merely as the erasure of physical obstacles: the restoration of safety and security in material life, which returns sick people to a container whose weaknesses have been repaired. Rather, they are challenging pictures of how illness, disability and death may become gateways to a greater, fuller life, a process in which the agency and empowerment of the healed person is always a central factor. These stories guide us toward finding the meaningful contents of life, toward beholding the spirit and joining the sacred dance.

My healing journey

My opportunity to make this transition and receive the gifts that come through illness arrived when I was in my late twenties. From childhood I had had disturbing inner experiences – paranoia, self-loathing, withdrawal, anxiety – but I had been able to keep these hidden. I never spoke of them to anyone, and they were never noticed by my peers or elders. My physical health was fairly robust; I only had a sensitive digestion that caused me to throw up easily in response to stomach bugs or motion sickness, and a tendency toward binge-eating and gaining excess weight.

I got through college successfully and seemed to be coping well enough in daily life. I had friends and a job teaching children in an elementary school, but I felt as though I were living behind a glass wall that shut me out from the world. Inside I was cold and numb, afraid to reveal my true self to anyone. Social situations made me extremely nervous and I shrank from public speaking or too much emotional engagement. Most disturbing to me was my apparent inability to love anyone deeply, and my occasional bouts of dissociation, which distanced me from my body and senses.

I was raised in a loving and secure family, so there was no obvious explanation for what might have caused me to have these experiences; I remained a mystery to myself. I was convinced there was something terribly wrong with me, that I was possibly evil and dangerous.

A light appeared in my darkness when I entered a part-time program in Seattle for learning about Waldorf education and its spiritual foundations in anthroposophy. Finally, experiences and ideas that had been isolated and incomprehensible began to fit together and make sense. Especially important was discovering how my individual destiny was a part of a greater arc of evolution that gave meaning to all the struggles human beings meet in life. It was something of a surprise to discover a Christian world view that included reincarnation, but after I had lived with this idea for a while it became one of the most important gifts anthroposophy brought me. I started to consider that what happened to me was not just random and arbitrary, nor part of a system of reward and punishment from some distant entity, but part of a learning process that I myself had had a role in shaping. This gave a different aspect to all the things I ordinarily most wanted to avoid, and slowly, over the course of many years, that began to change the way I thought and the choices I made.

Eurythmy was a particularly enlightening experience. I felt at once how invigorating it was to perform physical movements that were in accord with soul experiences – an expression of truth that was linked with human language but went far deeper into the very sources of meaning, into the *logos*. In eurythmy, word was truly made flesh.

I didn't at that time have any notion of entering the eurythmy training, but I was glad to have this source of enthusiasm appear in my formerly gray inner world. The course spoke to parts of me that had never been addressed before and helped me open up in unprecedented ways, although I still did not feel able to fully reveal myself.

I decided to enter the two-year full-time Waldorf teacher training at Sunbridge College (as it then was) in New York. I wasn't sure I wanted to be a Waldorf teacher, but I wanted to continue on this anthroposophical path somehow.

During my first year there, my inner life exploded. In place of numbness there appeared a confusing realm of uncontrollable emotions that could be exciting but also frightening. Unrequited romantic love caused overwhelming feelings of desire and dependency to surge up, then left me feeling even more paralyzed and numb. I hated my weakness and incapacity, which I saw as a lack of willpower and moral strength.

I started to have physical as well as psychological symptoms, such as backaches and sleeping problems. I was being challenged now to take up the gifts of illness, but I still did not tell anyone what I was going through, mainly out of shame and fear of rejection. I became convinced that what I truly loved was eurythmy and that switching to the eurythmy training would heal me. I even thought, in a surge of grandiosity, that it would help me to heal the world.

I expected the training to serve a first-half-of-life function: it would lead to a career and provide confirmation of my identity and a place in the world. I thought that 'healing' meant resolving the issues I'd been struggling with and returning to the peace and security I'd had before my problems began in childhood.

And I did find healing, but instead of the four years of the regular eurythmy training, it took more than twenty-five years and involved more illness and dysfunction, both inner and outer. It turned out that my first-half-of-life container needed more than just some minor fixes and superficial Band-Aids. It had to be practically destroyed and rebuilt, leading me through many kinds of death before I could reach the shores of life again. Only lately do I feel that I am reaching a kind of completion of that journey, assuming I can stop skipping over necessary steps or resisting needful death processes, thereby making the ordeal even longer.

I am grateful now for all that I have gone through, because I learned so much and came into contact with my true self, as well as into true, intimate relationships with other people. The precious fruit of all my suffering was that people became real to me, no longer just shadowy, symbolic figures in my inner drama. I also experienced the spiritual source of healing that is available to all human beings who are able to admit their need and reach out for it. My certain knowledge of this source of healing is more real than anything else I have ever experienced; it connects me to a firm ground of reality that I know will never pass away, no matter what storms may come. It doesn't mean that I have no more troubles or doubts or that all my symptoms are gone. They aren't. But whatever remains I can endure with patience, knowing that this, too, has something to teach me and will one day be turned to the good.

By sharing my story and my thoughts about the gospel healings in connection with it, I would like to encourage readers to bring their own need for healing to that infallible source of life and strength. It took me a long time to turn to it; I can only hope that by means of this sharing, someone else's way of suffering might be made shorter or lighter.

About this book

The healing stories in the gospels are not old news. They are patterns of energy and living forces that can still touch us today when we take them into our souls. Often, we encounter them in isolation, scattered through the liturgical readings of the church year or through other systems of Bible study. But when I started to read them in a more focused way a few years ago, it seemed to me that the order they were placed in was as significant as the stories themselves. Along with other events in the gospels, they could form a path of awakening leading up to the great event of Christ's crucifixion and resurrection, the beholding of which is meant to be the medicine for humanity's ills. This path could be followed by readers, allowing them to connect it to their own unique healing journey.

I started writing poems based on the healing stories during Advent, 2017. I was going through an extremely difficult time in my personal life, which included the possible end of my marriage, and during that contemplative season I decided to focus on the three instances of Jesus raising a person from death. I had no intention of writing poems, but that was the response my study produced. The stories were so short and cryptic that I needed to unfold them in my imagination and answer questions for myself about the lives of these people who had been raised to new life by Christ.

Four years later, after going through a huge crisis and moving with my family to Switzerland, I was faced with new physical challenges that culminated in gallbladder surgery. While recovering, I had an impulse to look at the healing stories again and perhaps write a few more poems. I did not know at first if I would complete the whole series, but after a while even the briefest and least relatable stories showed me a way into their world. Over about six months I wrote the remaining fifteen poems.

These poems felt like a gift that had opened up the gospel stories more fully for me, and I wondered if I could extend this gift to others. I decided to write background notes about some of the information I'd gathered in the course of writing the poems, and I added anecdotes from my life and healing journey that seemed to me to illustrate or complement the story in some way. Finally, I selected a sentence from each story that could be used as the basis for meditation or a prelude to silent contemplation.

This sequence shows how one might move from the reading of a given scriptural text to elaborating it with one's own ideas and research, either in a more artistic or a more discursive form. It then goes on to connect the text with one's personal experience and needs, and finally to concentrate it into a kind of meditative seed form. These stages are loosely based on the traditional practice of *Lectio Divina* or sacred reading, with its steps of reading, meditation (in the sense of pondering), prayer and contemplation.[3] It is a sequence that I've found helpful in engaging with these stories and with other passages from the Bible, but it is not the only way to do this.

The Gospel of Mark is thought by many textual scholars to be the earliest written down, and to have been a source for Luke and Matthew. Whether that is the case or not, it is notable that the stories of healing in this gospel are often the longest, even though it is the shortest of the three books. While it contains few of the parables and teachings found in Matthew and Luke, Mark devotes a relatively large amount of space and attention to healing. The stories in this gospel often contain significant details missing in the others, and have a unique arrangement with interesting features. For this reason it seemed to me appropriate to use Mark's sequence as a guiding principle. To this framework I added in the stories not found in Mark.

Although they are arranged very differently in some ways, certain healing events stretch across the Gospels of Matthew, Mark and Luke, known as the Synoptic Gospels. These healings stand as landmarks and turning points in a sequence of development. The table in Appendix 2 illustrates some of the similar and different ways the books are structured.

The Gospel of John is very different in both structure and content, and includes only three stories that bear some relationship to the healings in the other gospels, with the addition of the Raising of Lazarus as a crowning event.

It is beyond the scope of this book to go into all of the relationships between the four different accounts and their versions of the healing stories. In my notes I include a few observations that have been illuminating for me. I hope readers will be inspired to make their own discoveries.

And so, you are invited to enter with me upon the greatest adventure there can possibly be: the call to renewed life and creation that the gospels extend to every human being. Through reading the healing stories in the gospels, responding to them in poetry and prose writing, and reflecting on my personal life experiences in connection with them, I would like to provide a framework that may contribute to the unfolding of your own healing story. If it helps you or brings you further along in any way, that will give me the greatest joy.

Note: For those unfamiliar with the anthroposophical view of Christ and human evolution, some orientation may be helpful. Please see Appendix 1.

1.
A Man with an Unclean Spirit:
Mark 1:21–28

Rod of Iron

My father raised us
with the wisdom of Solomon –
he spared no rod
and spoiled no child.
He'd beat the demons out of us, he said,
make us pure and holy
and fearful of the Lord.

It didn't work with me.
Not fear, but rage grew as I grew,
flamed hot behind my eyes,
till one day, taller, stronger than him,
I snatched the rod
and broke it.

I threatened him with the splintered end
and I recall the surge of power
as he shrank from me,
diminished,
gone.

I'd dishonored our Law by dishonoring him,
but I didn't care.
I was old enough now to live on my own,
and I offered myself as a strongman, a builder,
to the soldiers who occupied our town.

I could work without tiring from sunrise to dark.
I could carry a whole beam on my shoulder,
and heave it in place, then go for another.
The work helped me silence the voices in my head,
the ones that said, '*Kill. Kill.*'

I was made foreman after a time.
I was good at whipping those lazy workers.
to frenzies of labor. My glares, my shouts,
and yes, if needed, the lash of my rod,
kept them moving, not daring to rest.

Once, I'd just finished with a man
who'd asked too many times for water,
left him bleeding and dripping his sweat in the dust,
when I saw it:
the sign against evil.

I should have flogged the man who made it,
but I pretended not to see,
shouted them all back to their work,
and worked myself like a man possessed,
pushing back the accusing voices,
the ones that said, '*Murderer.*'

But at night, in the dark, they rose again,
stood me before the judge's gaze,
and asked me what I'd made of myself.

I saw it.
I'd become *him*.

I was the demon I'd fought to escape,
and there was no hope, no way out of this prison.
We were locked in my body, forever.

The next day was Sabbath. I hadn't kept it
for many years, but this time I went,
crept in late to the synagogue,
stood at the back and listened.

I'd hear of God's cruelty, his hardness of heart,
how he punished and slew and tortured,
sent plagues and fire and famine,
and dropped men in the abyss.

There was a new rabbi I'd never seen.
He spoke not of rage, but forgiveness and love –
soft stuff, and yet his words were as iron.
They entered my soul, and flogged to death
the falseness I'd carried as God in me,
the lie that only in power was strength.

A great hope rose in my wounded boy's heart,
but I couldn't speak. The demons had my tongue,
and they wielded it like the lash of a whip,
taunting him with his likeness to them,
daring him to destruction,
confirming their hidden kinship.

Instead, he merely ordered their silence,
telling them to release the child
whose body they'd occupied so long.
My time of torment had come to an end;
the Master had entered the house.

I convulsed and cried and fell to the ground.
I thought I'd been killed,
but I'd go to my Father
a free man at last.

And it was a death, not for my body,
but for the man I had become.
I had to construct a new one.

I work for the synagogue now, hauling stones,
fixing cracks – whatever is needed to keep
the house of the Word ready when he comes.

He does come sometimes, and teaches again.
I always listen and rejoice
as on the day of my liberation.
But I fear there are many others who hear
yet are deaf to his word, still blinded by rage,
still captive to their own demons.

Will they not rest
until they have killed him?
And will we see then
how he wields his rod?

Reflections on *A Man with an Unclean Spirit*

In the Gospels of Mark and Luke, the first healing performed by Jesus is of a man with an unclean spirit. It is preceded by Jesus's teaching within a communal gathering of Jews, a synagogue. Before any healing of body or soul takes place, his words are described as having an unusual, indeed life-altering, power. Those who hear them are astonished, literally struck out of their wits (*ekplesso*[1]), and they identify Jesus as one who has authority (*exousia*), a ruler with the power to control and order events within a certain sphere.

In Mark, the significant word *eutheos* is used twice in this short episode. Usually translated as 'immediately' or 'at once', it connotes straightness and directness. It recalls the quotation from Isaiah which serves as the epigraph and leitmotif for this gospel: 'Prepare the way of the Lord; make straight [*euthus*] in the desert a highway for our God' (Isaiah 40:3). These are not outer paths; they are the ways of the human soul that have become crooked, distorted, unproductive and sick. The man with an unclean spirit appears 'immediately', straightaway, directly, as soon as Jesus begins teaching. The teacher's powerful words reveal what had remained hidden before; they cut through our defensive shields, as a surgeon's skill cuts through to the diseased organ.

The word for 'unclean' is *akathartos*. Modern psychology has familiarized us with the idea of catharsis: the need to dig out and work through past experiences that trouble our souls and disturb our physical health. Catharsis was the necessary first step of the ancient mysteries, for unaddressed impurities in the soul would lead to aberration and delusion when entering higher spheres of existence. In 'Rod of Iron' I have imagined an unhealed trauma that might have caused a man to appear to those around him as though he were possessed by a demon. There are countless examples of such phenomena in modern psychological case studies.[2]

Jesus 'rebukes' the demon. This verb, *epitimao*, is formed of the root *timao*, meaning 'to honor', and the prefix *epi-*, meaning 'upon' or 'against'. The primary meaning is to assess a penalty or set a just value upon something.[3] Christ is able to perceive the suffering soul and identify the correct response. It isn't a harsh, critical stance that he takes toward the sufferer, but that of a wise diagnostician who can see what is needed to restore balance. He rebukes the demon, not the man who suffers as a result of being possessed by the demon. In our time, when material science denies the existence of demons, we too often blame and judge people for behavior that is rooted in unhealed trauma. Unless we can learn to distinguish between a person's essential self and the forces of oppression and bondage that work against that self, we will not be able to heal anyone.[4]

The 'rod of iron' is an image given in Revelation 12:5, where the woman clothed with the sun is to give birth to a child who will 'rule [or shepherd] all the nations with a rod of iron.' And again, in Revelation 19:15 a rider on a white horse arrives to fight on behalf of humanity following a time of tribulation and suffering, and to rule or shepherd them with a rod of iron. This iron rod is a symbol of the true self, the ego, not in the sense of a rigid, petty self-centeredness, but representing that within us which is destined to become a just and good ruler if only we can straighten ourselves out and become firmly oriented toward spiritual truth. The iron rod is not the weapon of a tyrant; it is a shepherd's tool, a sign of protection and guidance. It seemed to me appropriate to point toward this image here, which represents the future potential of all those who are healed by Christ.

The demon's first words are difficult to translate. Literally they mean, 'What to you and to us, Jesus of Nazareth?' (Mark 1:24).

'What have you to do with us?' is one way to interpret this, but it remains a mysterious question. Almost the same phrase appears in the Gospel of John, at the Wedding at Cana: 'Woman, what to you and to me?' Jesus says to his mother (John 2:4).

In pondering this phrase, it seemed to me that one way to understand it is as a question about what two entities have in common. At Cana, at the beginning of his ministry, Jesus has only recently become the vessel for the Christ. The human sheaths of Jesus have received the immense cosmic content of this great being, who is in a way still to be born. He experiences a period of gestation within Jesus at this point (as he says to his mother at the wedding, 'My hour has not yet come.'). This is similar to when Mary consented to bear Jesus, an act of humble service and receptivity to a greater being. The gesture of opening up to a loving, divine power is what moves between and within Jesus and his mother, and it becomes active as the force that turns water into wine.

When they recognize the Christ being within Jesus, the demons say, 'What to you and to us?' ('What do you have to do with us?'). Perhaps they are asking if he is going to act as they do: overpowering and manipulating the sheath within which they dwell in an attempt to deprive their human host of his freedom. Christ could certainly do this. He could master the demons and take their place, forcing humans to be good through his overwhelming power, but he doesn't. Instead, he will condense and adapt his might more and more to his human bearer until he is even able to die as a human being. This is not something the demons can understand, alien as it is to their will to dominate and control.

The selflessly creative word of Christ is more powerful than theirs: he silences their words of evil, thereby ending their power over the human they have held in thrall all this time.

In Matthew, Jesus's initial teaching activity is represented by the Sermon on the Mount (chapters 5–7), which ends with the same phrase that introduces this healing in the other two Synoptic Gospels: '[They] were astonished at his teaching, for he was teaching them as one who had authority, and not as their scribes' (Matthew 7:28–29). I would venture that the entire Sermon on the Mount is closely related to the healing of the man with an unclean spirit, which is not otherwise described in Matthew. As Jesus teaches his disciples upon the heights of the mountain, he offers them the opportunity to cleanse their spirits and make 'straight the paths' in themselves that will enable them in turn to be healers. We, too, can be cleansed and redirected to our true selves when we take in these words.

One powerful image near the end of the Sermon on the Mount is that of the beam that we must cast out of our own eye before we can see clearly to help others (Matthew 7:3).[5] The word used here for casting out is the same used elsewhere for casting out a demon: *ekballo*. Again, cleansing ourselves of the negative effects of buried trauma, bringing the light of compassionate understanding to bear upon all that presents as frightening and repulsive in human behavior, is the essential healing activity that we can enter into when we follow the way of Christ. Then we will experience the divine being who condemns no one and seeks instead to restore all of humanity to their true and essentially good way of being.

Personal Connections – Part 1

When I was twenty-one years old, I had an out-of-body experience.

Nobody knew this at the time. Back then I was, outwardly, a normal college student. I had friends, achieved good grades, and showed potential for the future. But inside I had developed an inner coldness and a numbness that I didn't know how to overcome. I hid myself, fearful of judgment and criticism, and I compensated in my usual way: I did what made people happy, I was successful in school, and I kept my real thoughts and feelings to myself.

It was my last semester in college and I was growing impatient with myself. I had still to enter into life, and in late-twentieth-century college culture, that meant one thing: sex. I was a virgin, and therefore a freak. I'd had crushes on guys, but none had ever been interested in me except as a friend, and the few who wanted me had only made me want to run away. But I thought I needed to be less picky and so, assisted by the disinhibiting influence of alcohol, I got closer to one classmate who had indicated he liked me.

When it came to physical contact, though, something terrible happened. I felt as though I were outside of my body, watching it walk around and doing things I didn't want it to do, while I felt helpless to stop it. Before things went too far, I cut off the relationship without telling this young man or anyone else what I had experienced. I was terrified by this distance that yawned between me and my body, by the way it had taken on an independent life of its own.

If I wasn't in my body, then what was? Could something get into it that way and use it? Wouldn't that be evil? Or was this dissociation a sign of psychosis?

I hadn't felt any pleasure or desire in our contact, only numbness and repulsion, confirming my worst fears that I was an unnatural, cold, loveless, frigid person. No one must ever know how abnormal I was, I thought.

The problem, however, did not go away. It reappeared in my next venture, a graduate program where I would earn a master's degree and certificate in elementary education. I'd applied to this program sight unseen and been accepted on the basis of my excellent grades and high test scores, but I soon learned that good test scores do not a good elementary school teacher make. I hadn't been around children other than my younger siblings since my own childhood; I had vague, high-minded ideas that all the boredom and bullying I'd endured as a child could be cured by more progressive, more imaginative forms of education, and that these would be perfectly simple to implement. They were just waiting for innovators like me to enter the classroom.

I was not prepared for the reality of a room full of squirming, chattering, uncontrollable third graders, or for the nervous terror they would inspire in me. Once more I was knocked out of my body, unable even to see what was in front of my face. I had an actual experience of blacking out while still standing up and walking around. Here was the numbness and dissociation, my hidden monster, jumping out to ambush me again.

I didn't tell anyone. After one disastrous lesson in which I was supposed to teach the multiplication tables but ended up with a room in chaos, the teacher who was mentoring me had to step in and take over. Afterwards, she asked me to explain what had happened. Why had I done nothing to address the disruption in the ways we had already discussed?

I couldn't tell her the truth, which was that I hadn't even been aware of it. I was so caught up in the storm of fear and anxiety inside me that I had become blind and deaf to the children and the classroom. I couldn't say that, for it would show how deficient I really was.

And what would happen then? Would I be thrown out of the program? Would I fail?

I'd never failed in school before in my life.

I stammered something about just not knowing what to do.

Patiently, the teacher went back over what my options had been, explaining the principles of discipline and order that make for a well-run classroom. We made a plan for what I could do better next time.

And I did get better.

I learned some strategies and tools to help me cope, and avoided losing my vision completely in the classroom. The children were darlings, really, and they gave me their affection along with their naughty tricks. After some better experiences, I grew more comfortable with them. At the end of the semester, my teacher said I'd done a fine job with the last unit on the geography and cultures of Mexico, and so I was able to relax a bit and enjoy our final celebration – a Mexican fiesta!

I went on to teach in Montessori elementary schools for a few years, and then later pursued Waldorf teacher training. But that disconnection remained, hidden and unspeakable. Eventually my body started to protest, speaking up through the physical health issues that impelled me into the eurythmy training.

Now I know that it is trauma which pushes people out of their bodies and keeps them from connecting to the world, causing such feelings of numbness and dissociation. And I have also learned that trauma does not have to be outwardly, physically perceptible, as with a child who is beaten by their parents. It can occur on much subtler levels, and it can sometimes be impossible to identify a perpetrator. There may be no one to blame, no one to judge. There is only a life process that over the generations has fallen out of balance as we try to survive in an environment that has grown ever more toxic to our most essential nature.

But at the time, I had no idea that the wrongness I felt was a condition, not a characteristic. Rather than understanding that something had happened to me, and to all of humanity, I thought there was something wrong with me. I judged myself. I was terrified of others rejecting me, and therefore pre-empted them by rejecting myself. At least that way I was somewhat in control.

But being in control is not living. Clinging to our defense mechanisms keeps us from entering into the true life that Christ offers us – that's why his way has to lead through death. It may only be the death of our illusions and our fears, but it is still no small matter to give up those defenses, when we believe they are all that stands between us and annihilation.

I can feel for the man possessed by demons, whose own voice was stolen from him by some inhuman power, while they took over his body and made use of it. And I can sense the relief of being met by Christ, who perceives the difference between that power and the oppressed individual. He is able to separate them out and give back to the oppressed human ego the ability to stand up and speak its truth.

At that time, I did not yet put together the Gospel of Christ with my own need for healing. For me, religion was still connected with my outer persona that strove to be 'good', and not with my secret shame and my experience of abject failure and wrongness. I couldn't admit to that underside, least of all in church. The defenses had to come down still further, but they would eventually fall. And then I would see that the Healer had been there all along, waiting for me.

> *Meditation*
> Be silent, and come out of him.

2.
A Woman with a Fever:
Mark 1:29–31

Fisher of Men

I wasn't born to this, you know –
this peasant dwelling, stinking of fish.
And nor was my daughter; she ought to be
a queen, I thought, or wife to some lord,
not scraping scales and mending nets
in a backwater town by the sea.

He's a good man, I know. Too good for me,
no doubt, and better than any I'd cause
to hope for, after what happened to mine.
The swords, the screams, the spill of blood –
I can't speak of it.
You know.

It was afterward that the fevers began.
My heat would rise, and I'd be a forest
consumed by flame. I'd shriek and mutter,
raging against those vipers and wolves,
till the fire left me a blackened stump
ready to fall to ash.

I was glad of the heat, for otherwise
the fear made me so cold.

But it worried my daughter.
When they wed her off
to this Simon, this nameless nobody,
she begged him to take us far away,
away from that poisoned court.

So here we are, by the great lake shore.
But the water could not cool my mad heart
or keep me from burning.
I still shook and flamed
and collapsed into dark
till they feared for my life.

He entered the house as a cooling wind,
laden with rain, soothes summer's heat.
The sea was still, awaiting his word.
The very fish were watching.

And his hand was cool, not cold like a fish,
but cool with a hidden warmth within
that sought out my heat and released it, diffused it,
allowed it to enter an endless sky
and be breathed away.
The smoke drifted off
and the air was clear.

He said no word.
He didn't have to – I knew him.
This was the one the men chatter about.
Their teacher, their leader,
who's called them off
to leave their nets and become even poorer,
losing what little they have.

What folly, I'd thought.
But now I knew:
this was the One,
the healer, the hope,
the only chance
for a burning world
to be saved from ending in ash.

I didn't tell my son-in-law.
Let him learn for himself.
Those men think themselves
so clever, so wise.

Someday they will know
what women see at once
but can never say,
except through our bodies –
through their flaming, their falling,
the fiery seeds that float in us,
cycling through death and rebirth.

I can't say these words;
they won't listen to me.
But they will hear him.
He will speak it.
He will show it.
He will live it,
and die it.

So I can wait.
I'll serve them in silence,
my flame settled down,
tamed to a hearth-fire
that keeps me warm
and safe from the wolves.

Maybe I'll marry again. I'm still
a young woman, you know.
I can leave the fish too,
the boats and the nets,
and fish for a man of my own.

Reflections on *A Woman with a Fever*

In researching this text I came across little that was helpful in identifying the mysterious woman with a fever; most commentators seem to think she represented an anonymous, insignificant housewife. I find that unlikely, however. Surely 'Simon's mother-in-law' indicates someone of significance whose own name could not be mentioned for some reason. Perhaps it was a mystery formula of some kind, or she was a politically important person who could only be talked about in a sidelong way.

The only interesting theory I found, based on a dubious identification with a man named 'Cephas' in another ancient text, argued that Peter had formerly served in the household of Bernice, the wife of Herod the Great's son Aristobolus. The legend is that Peter married the daughter of Herod's other son, Alexander, thus making Peter's mother-in-law Glaphys, Alexander's Jewish wife.[1]

Herod had both his sons murdered because he was afraid they were plotting to take his throne. This would explain why Glaphys ended up as a poor fisherman's relative, Peter having found fishing preferable to staying in the poisonous court of the Herods.

Glaphys was known for constantly gossiping, complaining and stirring things up, and probably contributed to the death of her own husband with her meddling and inflammatory words. She had affairs and married again, not just once but several times. And yet in the middle of all this scandal and notoriety she managed to get healed by Jesus in Galilee.

It's a far-fetched story, but it was fun to consider it as a possibility. In the absence of any other explanation, it provides at least some key to the puzzle of who Peter's mother-in-law was and why she comes into the story so briefly and yet so significantly.

The three short descriptions of this event in the Synoptic Gospels have small but important differences that point to different qualities. In Mark, that significant word *eutheos* ('straightaway', 'immediately') is used twice in two successive sentences. The straight path humanity needs to recover is indicated again. When Jesus takes the woman by the hand and raises her up, the word used is *egeiro*. The same expression can be used for awaking from sleep or rising from the dead. In recovering from the fever that paralyzes her soul with an excessive, out-of-control warmth, she rises as if from a deathbed, a prelude to other resurrection stories in the gospels.

In Matthew, Jesus merely touches her hand, but the verb 'to touch', *hapto*, also means to kindle a fire. In place of her raging fever, a new kind of warmth has been kindled through the Christ encounter. In Luke, Christ 'rebukes' (*epitimao*) the fever. As in the story of the demon-possessed man, he assesses the right treatment for this woman whose inner fire has gone out of control.

In conventional modern medicine, fever and acute inflammation are treated as enemies that must be suppressed. Meanwhile, chronic inflammation is rampant and increasing, due to toxic conditions on many levels that cause our stress response to become stuck in the 'on' position. This inflammation plays a role in many illnesses, from diabetes to auto-immune disorders to depression.[2]

The rightful purpose of inflammation is to assist in a process of transformation and rebalancing. It should be a temporary state that helps to loosen up things that need to change. In a blog post on inflammation, Dr Adam Blanning writes, 'An essential part of health is that our body has the flexibility to loosen and shift and change to a new state as needed.'[3] Fever, he says, needs to be supported to properly complete this process without becoming a danger in itself. He points out that there are times when provoking an acute illness can help to heal a chronic illness (researchers are experimenting with using the measles vaccine to provoke the immune system to clear out cancer cells, for example). Dr Blanning goes on to say that 'being healthy does not mean that we never get sick'. The transformative processes of illness can therefore be very important for reaching a new level of health.

In my poem about Christ's touching and raising of the woman with a fever, I've imagined a chronic inflammation process being brought to resolution, which leads to transformation and the taking on of a new role. In the Synoptic Gospels, the woman rises and begins to serve Jesus and the disciples. Our illnesses are actually servants of our greater health when they come into right relationship with the higher wisdom that guides our lives.

No other relative of a disciple is identified as having such an encounter with Christ. And it amused me to imagine that this nameless woman might have outpaced her famous son-in-law by having insight into the nature of her healer well before Peter's own recognition of the Messiah (see Matthew 16:16, Mark 8:29 and Luke 9:20).

Although women's voices in the gospels may often go unheard, their silent power of perception and lived experience forms the subtext to much of what takes place through Jesus's ministry. Healing cannot happen unless we integrate this feminine experience with the more light-filled, conscious, masculine faculty that is accessible to us through language and linear thinking. In other words, we need both Peter and his mother-in-law, whoever she may be.

Personal Connections – Part 2

My first real encounter with Christ took place in the toilet.

I was twenty-three years old and living in my first apartment, which I was sharing with a friend from college after I'd finished my master's program and moved back to the Seattle area where I'd grown up. By the end of our year in the tiny, slant-roofed attic space, my friend had found a boyfriend and basically moved in with him, leaving me alone in the apartment most of the time. I decided to move to a house my parents had just bought in the city.

I was therefore responsible for the moving-out process, but I had no idea what was involved or expected in moving out of an apartment. I'd never had to clean anything in my life; my mother had done it in our house, and in college I had always lived in dorms with housekeeping services. When my friend was still there, we had split the duties of wiping counters and vacuuming, keeping things reasonably tidy.

I suppose she was also the one who cleaned the bathroom, because after she left the toilet was never scrubbed. If I noticed the bowl growing browner, it did not occur to me to pick up a brush or do anything about it. So accomplished in school, I was helpless in practical matters. I was too ashamed to ask anyone for help. My mind darted away from anything that provoked doubt and anxiety, creating areas of blindness that were supposed to keep me safe, but really just crippled and limited me.

On the day I moved out, I gathered up my things, did what I thought was sufficient cleaning, and then left. I had a vague idea that maybe something more was expected of me, but I'd be gone. Our landlady, trusting us, had already given us back our security deposit. I'd never have to see her again, I thought.

That night the phone rang in my new house. Unsuspectingly, I picked it up.

'Hello?' I said.

A storm of rage and accusation assaulted me down the phone line, an inarticulate yelling that at first I could not understand. Then I got it. My landlady had gone upstairs to inspect the apartment.

'How could you?! A brown toilet! I trusted you, I gave you back your deposit…' I stopped hearing complete sentences, only angry words that battered my ears: 'Dirty… filthy… disgusting…'

The apartment was dirty. *I* was dirty. I was a filthy, disgusting mess. The accusation wounded me.

I hadn't meant to be bad! I was a *good* girl, always doing what was expected of me, getting good grades, pleasing my elders. I hadn't known about cleaning toilets. My landlady was the bad one, yelling at me like this, not letting me explain. Was she drunk? She sounded drunk. Her speech sounded slurred, her behavior was irrational. I hated her! She was the evil one, not me.

I managed to stammer something about being sorry, I would make sure the apartment was cleaned, and got her to hang up. I huddled in my bed and wrestled with the shock of it.

I let the hatred for my landlady fill me up, flaming inwardly with rage at her in return for her accusations. All the anger that my numbness had been covering up for years roared up like a fire suddenly bursting through a wall. It was her fault, not mine!

Hate, hate, hate!

But this hatred was consuming me, not helping me. It gnawed at me like a dog at a bone. How could I counter it? How could I find peace?

I didn't ever pray, and I hadn't gone regularly to church during my college years, but I prayed now:

'Christ, help me!'

And suddenly, I could see things from my landlady's point of view. I could see what a shock it must have been to enter the apartment expecting it to be clean (after all, those nice girls, so quiet and unobtrusive), and instead finding a brown toilet! Had it not been cleaned for months?

No, it hadn't. I hadn't known I was supposed to do that, but now I did and I had to accept responsibility. It wasn't right for her to rage at me like that, but I had to admit that I had done something wrong as well.

Calling on Christ had brought this change in my perspective. It had allowed me to come out of my narrow self and connect to a greater whole, to understand that other people were real and had rights and feelings of their own just as I did. It was hard to admit my own wrongdoing, but it was necessary. I was part of a larger world and taking my place in it meant that I had to expand my awareness beyond my particular point of view. I had the strength to do that now. I could go on without being torn apart by my rage and frustration.

I owed that to Christ. I knew I could not have done it all by myself.

Deeply shaken by this experience, I called my roommate and asked if she would help me clean the apartment. I couldn't possibly face the landlady again, even if I had forgiven her for attacking me. Instead, my friend generously agreed to finish the cleaning herself. I don't know what she thought when she saw the toilet. We drifted apart and I lost touch with her after that.

I tried to forget the whole incident as soon as possible, although I did learn how to clean a toilet. It would not turn brown in my new place.

It was a long time before I could talk about this experience and even laugh at myself, at my own naïve, clueless behavior. I was still fearful of being judged and found deficient; I was unwilling to show my 'dirt' in public. But I knew that Christ had seen it, and his hand had touched me with acceptance and restored me to life and community. Though the experience faded, and I had no sense of his constant presence, no desire or ability to keep praying, I knew that my experience had been spiritually real. Even if such a thing never happened again, that one incident had an indelible force that I could not deny or forget. It became a riddle at the back of my mind that I had to solve.

In Peter's nameless mother-in-law, I see my own feverish passions immobilizing me as if on a deathbed. And with her, I can feel how the touch of Christ calms my flaming ego and enables me to see how our lives are most fully lived in service of others. This does not mean losing my dignity and independent worth as I wallow in the consciousness of my shame. It means that I am one ego among many, and I need to take responsibility for the wrong I do, while maintaining respect and compassion when I am wronged by others.

We all wound each other in some way, and we need a mediating helper to enable us to make reparation, to clean up our mess. The dirt and mess had been piling up in me for a long time, but with just this hint of a helper, I could take some steps toward cleansing that accumulation.

> *Meditation*
>
> And he came and took her by the hand
> and lifted her up, and the fever left her,
> and she began to serve them.

3.
A Leper:
Matthew 8:1–4

Made Clean

You know those dreams
you can't shake on waking –
those fogs of the mind
that leave you unsure
of the line between self and other.
Was that my own voice, or was it an angel
calling me to deeds of brightness,
a prophet's inspiration?
Or was it rather some darker spirit
sent to test my sense of truth,
luring me onto false paths?
The colors mix and blend, they shift
and interpenetrate, confusing,
deceiving the eye of the soul.

And so with this fog of the skin, which blurs
the boundary that sets us apart,
makes us human, not plants or stones,
marks us as kin to God.
A mist creeps over what should be clear,
obscuring it, mixing up self and world,
making our flesh unguarded and raw,
destroying our sacred shield.

Such a shieldless man, Moses decreed,
cannot remain in community,
any more than a tent or a robe or a wall
so weak and corrupted can be kept.
If it can't be cleansed, it must be destroyed,
must return to the elements it's made of.

Our mercy is not to kill such men,
but to cast them out, throwing them
into the arms of a wilderness God,
letting them walk, as Moses did,
on the borderline between slave and free,
and maybe be burned into life.

It was so with me. When I saw the spot,
how it spread, how it ate away my surface,
I knew I was marked for loneliness
and exile, far from home.
Maybe, away from the world, I'd discover
what it really is that makes us men,

not our fragile skin or brittle bones,
but something inside us, deeper than blood.

I could not find it by myself.
pushed to the edge, alone and unclean,
I knew only the dread of my stopless disease,
until I saw him. He'd just come down
from a mountain, like Moses, aflame with God,
where he'd fired dull hearts with the will of creation,
speaking them back to humanity.

And I knew that this was what I sought.
If I opened myself, my poor, raw flesh,
to his healing will, I'd be restored.
His openness was all to the Father,
his shield all against our Enemy.

I knelt, and prayed,
and he made me clean,
cleansed by the uncorrupted Word
that speaks us back to communion.

He gave me his skin
to cover my wounds,
his garment embracing us all,
his shelter in which we are one:
one human body,
one divine love.

No longer an exile.
nor a slave,
I was home at last,
and free.

Reflections on A Leper

The rules for how to diagnose and treat skin diseases are found in Leviticus, chapters 13 and 14. These elaborate conditions are some of the strangest and most difficult for us to relate to today, and yet they occupy a prominent place in the Torah. Elsewhere in the Hebrew scriptures, physical cleanness is used as a metaphor for moral cleanness and is equated with worthiness to serve and encounter God:

> Who shall ascend the hill of the Lord? And who shall stand in His holy place? He who has clean hands and a pure heart, who does not lift up his soul to what is false and does not swear deceitfully. (Psalm 24:3–4)

The cleansing of skin disease was a religious matter because all outer disease and dysfunction could be a sign of inner disease. In the Israelites' intensely communal life, neither could be permitted to fester and spread.

But distancing ourselves from disease, though it may be necessary for a time, is not the ultimate solution. Physical or psychological illness has the potential to become a pathway to spiritual insight if we respond to it in the right way, and that possibility is also represented in the Hebrew Bible. In the story of Job, thought to be the most ancient text in the Bible, Job must undergo many trials, including his skin being afflicted with boils. His suffering, which is exacerbated by the baseless accusations of his so-called friends that he must be guilty of something, brings him to the point of grasping divine truth: 'For I know that my Redeemer lives, and at the last he will stand upon the earth' (Job 19:25). This may be understood as a foreshadowing of the way of Christ, which involves a blameless person enduring extreme suffering in order to bring higher forces into play within the earth.

While on the difficult path of enduring suffering, we need help and companionship. If we are cast out and left alone, we can feel a great need for a divine Friend. The essence of the Good News, the Gospel, is that this Friend has arrived and now 'stands upon the earth'. He makes himself known to the suffering leper through his willingness to touch him – something no devout adherent to the Holiness Code in Leviticus would have dared to do. Christ's will is to be near us, to be like us, to share our suffering and even our diseases. That companionship, that compassion, is a healing force that restores the wholeness we have lost.

The positioning of the leper's healing is interesting. In Mark, the first healings directly follow the calling of the first disciples, and they are in the order I've used in this book: a man with an unclean spirit, a woman with a fever, a leper. Right before the healing of the leper, there is a description of how Jesus widens his ministry from Capernaum into all of Galilee, and how crowds begin to seek and follow him.

In Luke, the calling of the disciples does not take place until after Jesus has begun his ministry of teaching and performed the first two individual healings. The healing of the leper is the first to be described after the disciples are chosen. In Matthew, it is the first individual healing described. It takes place immediately after the Sermon on the Mount, after Jesus has descended from the mountain and great crowds have begun to follow him, attracted by the power he has displayed as he teaches his disciples. I've made reference to this in the poem.

The healing of the leper therefore seems to have a special connection to discipleship, to the call to follow a healer and become a healer oneself. For Christ, this does not involve holding oneself apart, seeking purity and cleanliness in isolation or through the repudiation of undesirable elements. The will of the divine healer is to touch what is unclean, to make whole again what has been sundered and fragmented. Human individualization was a necessary step toward freedom, but now is the time to mend what was broken, to restore the outcast to the community.

The work of Christ Jesus with the disciples is directed toward showing them how they can be co-workers with him in this great task. The healings are lessons for them, living parables to transform their thoughts in a healing direction. We, too, as students and disciples of the Christ impulse, can follow this path of instruction, finding a new way to relate to all that we would otherwise recoil from, all that is unclean, diseased or contaminated in us and in our world.

Personal Connections – Part 3

A few years after my Christ-encounter in the toilet, I discovered anthroposophy and fell in love with eurythmy. Desperate to prove that I could love something, I threw my usual caution to the wind and committed to training in eurythmy. But I soon discovered that I was not a successful student anymore. I was unable to keep up with the rest of the class. I had no energy for practicing, especially for the solos. These left me feeling empty and drained, unsupported by the energy of the rest of the group. In the second year I had a serious bout of depression that took me out of class for weeks, and the physical symptoms I thought would be resolved by the training only shifted to new areas and got worse. The teachers didn't know much about what was going on in my inner life, but they could see that something was wrong in the way that I moved and so they insisted I have extra tutoring. It didn't help.

My teachers seemed to think that describing the problems they saw would be enough to help me overcome them. They told me my movements were stiff and lacking in fullness, broken at the elbows and wrists. Eurythmy did not flow through me; I was too heavy and earthbound. My speech and my thinking, as well as my movements, were cutting and sharp. My teachers told me that I 'knew too much' and that I needed to become more innocent, like a little child.

'You don't seem to be able to use your body as an instrument,' one of them said.

My shameful, secret inadequacy was uncovered; I'd been given away by my own body. It was a relief, in a way. But I couldn't just suddenly 'be lighter' as the teachers told me to be. They spoke as if their command were the magic spell that would cure me, but how could it be effective to tell students to do things they could not do?

Surely teaching had to start with what a student could do and grow from there.

But was there anything I could do?

If I was not able to use my body as an instrument, not just to do eurythmy but to manifest my own creative spirit in any way, then I was a broken person and ought to be discarded. I'd be better off dead. Whenever I inwardly caught a glimpse of my brokenness – the ugly, parasitic weakness of my disconnected being – I had the urge to cast it out, to end it all by seeking oblivion.

Yet something kept me from taking that step, some thread of awareness that told me self-destruction was not the answer.

I began to feel angry at my teachers for not understanding what I was going through, but I couldn't talk about my real feelings; I hardly knew them myself. The numbness in my inner life had been replaced by a confusing swirl of emotions and compulsive thoughts. Bleak, hopeless depression alternated with grandiose ideas of my own superiority that eventually drained away, leaving me exhausted and limp again.

There was just one time, as I was crying in the dressing room after a solo showing, when a teacher took the time to ask if I needed support and advised me to talk to a counselor or doctor. Somehow, I needed that permission from an authority figure before I could seek help; I was unable to do it out of myself, no matter how bad my symptoms became. Looking back, I owe so much to that gesture of compassion; I truly don't know what would have happened to me, otherwise.

I did start to work with an anthroposophical doctor, and though my physical and emotional ailments (headaches, sleeping problems, body aches, menstrual problems, anger attacks) didn't abate much, at least I felt I could talk honestly with him. He didn't judge me or make pronouncements about my ability to do anything. Instead, he gave me a different perspective on my perceived deficiency, not seeing it as a sign that something was wrong with *me*, but merely with the way my 'parts' were put together. Some shock or trauma had pushed my upper members (my ego and soul body) out of my lower members (my physical and life body).

Because of this shock some dark, unpenetrated thing kept rising up and disturbing my inner and outer organism. 'There's something you don't want to face,' the doctor said matter-of-factly. That made sense. But what was the thing I didn't want to face, and why was it so difficult? I didn't know, but just the idea that my sickness was a condition, a disjunction of parts, rather than some indelible characteristic of my essential being, gave me some relief.

Like Job, I had to struggle to stay connected to some blameless essence within myself, the part of me whose connection to God was not disrupted even as my outwardly visible condition deteriorated. But my sense of the Redeemer who would stand by me in this struggle was still faint and elusive.

After my third year of eurythmy training, I was told I was not making enough progress and would have to repeat a year of the curriculum. During that summer, feeling discouraged and hopeless about my future, I began attending the services of the Christian Community. I'd been to the communion service once before, when I first arrived in Spring Valley, but it had just been a lot of meaningless words. Now, invited by a friend to come along with her to New York City, I went again, not expecting much. I sat in the service and listened to the words, and even though I didn't consciously take in any more of their content than before, I felt something new. As I watched the priest go through the ritual of offering and transubstantiation, and as I received the communion, I felt, *This is real*. Real spiritual substance was being prepared in this service, and it was being given to me if I was willing to receive it. I was being offered a key to reality, a little piece of the firm ground that eluded me in my inner and outer life.

There was no question that I wanted to take this up. More than anything I needed to get a grip on reality and find a firm place to stand in the middle of the raging storm of conflicting thoughts and feelings.

I started to go to the service as often as I could, catching a ride with others who made the drive to New York every week. I took in the words more and more, slowly understanding them with both my mind and my heart. The service was beautiful, I realized, a kind of poetry that lifted ordinary words to a higher level. It was like a magic spell that could undo ugly transformations and turn things back into what they really are. Even though the sacrament still contained many puzzling unknowns, I knew taking part in it was a good thing for me to do. It was like a medicine I sorely needed and that I could be treated with for a long time.

I went to the communion service, the Consecration of the Human Being, for several months. Then I asked the priest if I could have another, private sacrament, the Sacrament of Consultation, which consists of one or more conversations with the priest, and a special prayer. I don't remember exactly what I said, but I must have talked mainly about my difficulties in the eurythmy training, all the hard things I was hearing from the teachers, my weakness and incapacity.

I didn't know beforehand what the prayer would be about. It turned out to be about love. It spoke of what a human being had to do to experience being filled with love for God and all other human beings. The first word of the prayer was 'Learn'.

In my eurythmy training, I was being told that I was incapable of learning. And in myself I had long felt incapable of love. But with this prayer I discovered that, despite this apparent incapacity, God had not given up on me. God still thought that I could learn, and that I could love. I could overcome the shameful inadequacy that had plagued me for so many years and that had become visible to others through my clumsiness in eurythmy. I had only to come into a right relationship with the divine, offering up my thoughts, receiving grace to guide me in my will. Then my soul would feel peace.

Peace! What was more elusive for my tormented soul? If only I could reach this promised land, this haven.

I knew it would take time. I didn't expect an instant, magic solution, as I once had. But it was something I could work on. I had been shown a way.

Like the leper in the story, my status at the eurythmy school was of someone suffering from an incurable condition, who could only be kept at a distance and eventually exiled if the known modes of therapy did not work. And I had always gone along with that pattern: denying and exiling any weakness that came to my attention. With that attitude, neither my own will nor the will of the teachers was enough to address what ailed me.

Through the sacraments, however, something of another order of being started to work in me: not an alien will taking over my own, but something that enabled my own fragile, overwhelmed will to wake up and begin to be active again. Like a scaffolding within which I could take down a broken building and begin to reconstruct it, the sacraments helped me to start the process of cleansing and repair.

Meditation

Lord, if you will, you can make me clean.

4.
An Invalid by the Pool of Bethesda:
John 5:1–18

The Pool

It's by the Sheep Gate, the first to be built,
where the sacred lambs are led to slaughter,
that the wandering ones of Israel
might find their way back to the fold.

Near that Gate, you'll find a pool
where the sacrifice is cleansed before dying,
and where human sinners languish
awaiting healing or death.

From my boyhood it fascinated me,
this groaning reservoir of pain,
the piled-up weight of suffering
that only an angel could lift.

I started to spend all my time there,
turned my back on family and friends,
devoted myself to the needy sinners,
helping them into the pool.

When the angel would come and trouble the waters
at first the air just felt a bit brighter.
Heads lifted – eager, charged with hope
that this time would be their turn.

Then the surface would start to tremble
and bubbles rise from far below
till the whole pool heaved and shuddered
like a boiling cauldron of doom.

By then it would be too late to move.
You've got to be already in the pool
when the turmoil hits, or else you miss it –
the change has passed you by.

So I helped them. As soon as I felt the air
from the angel's wings, I chose my target,
lifted, dragged, or led him down
to the holy water's edge.

Oh, how they leapt with joy and wonder!
They thanked me, and left – back to their friends,
their families, all that welcoming life,
and I smiled and hugged my pride.

Until the day when I was struck down.
The angel approached – and I couldn't move!
I was stuck to my pallet, a groaning one now,
helpless and stiff with rage.

All the people I'd saved had forgotten me.
No family, no friends – surrounded by those
I hadn't chosen, the overlooked ones.
They watched me with blank, silent eyes.

Too proud to say 'Help!' I lay there, alone.
For nigh forty years, I watched the water,
watched as the crippled and blind and weak
struggled into the pool.

They didn't need my help. They did it
all by themselves, somehow from within
finding the strength, the will to move,
the angel that rose up in them.

But I couldn't do it. I lay there, lamed
by my years of being a useless crutch
instead of a father, a giver of life;
I'd chosen this tomb for myself.

Then he came – not an angel, a man.
He walked into my five-doored tomb,
like one who knew full well what he sought,
like an architect taking its measure.

He saw me at once. Really saw – he knew
who I was, what I'd done, how foolish and weak
my fruitless will had made me, how sad
that I couldn't help myself.

'Do you want to be healed?' he asked, and the years
boiled up in my throat, a wave of rage
and loneliness, and fear. My heart
was troubled, unsettled, changed.

Then it stilled, and I could tell the truth:
'I've no one to help me. I'm all alone.
I left life, and now it has left me.
I lie here on my deathbed, I know.'

He smiled, and in his eyes I saw
the hope I'd only sensed before,
the Word whose stirring once shaped the earth
now somehow speaking in us.

It said: 'Rise up, take your bed, and walk.'
So I did. It wasn't hard, after that.
I only had to let the hope lift me
and settle its spring in my heart.

I lost sight of him then, in the surging crowd
who wanted to celebrate my healing,
surprising me with their outburst of joy,
immersing me back into life.

When he found me again, I knew that his way
is not for those who refuse to taste death,
who cling to their pallets of righteousness
and won't admit they are ill.

He warned me, as I tried to warn them,
those others who want to help everyone else.
But they were tightly bound to their beds,
unable to stand his word.

I hear they want to kill him now.
Kill that one? Well, I suppose they can try,
but they might be astonished by what bursts forth.
I'll just sit by his water, and wait.

Reflections on An Invalid by the Pool of Bethesda

In the Gospel of John, the account of the healing that inspired 'The Pool' has several notable differences from a related story in the other gospels. In the Synoptic Gospels, a strong community element is expressed. A paralyzed man is brought to Jesus by his friends, who help to lower him through the roof of the house where Jesus is preaching to a large crowd. In John, however, the man has no friends who can help him into the pool. When Jesus asks him if he wants to be healed, the man's reply indicates that he can't do it by himself: 'I have no one to help me into the pool when the water is stirred' (John 5:7). His loneliness, in comparison to the communal support pictured in the other version of the story, also serves to highlight the other difference between them, namely their setting. The account given in Matthew, Mark and Luke takes place in Galilee, whereas in John it is in Judea, at the entrance to Jerusalem.

In *The Three Years*, Emil Bock vividly describes the difference between Galilee and Judea, and makes it clear that these are soul realms with diametrically opposite qualities. Galilee, where most of the healings in the Synoptic Gospels take place, is a fertile land rich in natural powers of growth and regeneration, centered around a living sea full of fish. By contrast, journeying into Judea brings us to the desert and to the shores of the Dead Sea where nothing can live. But as Bock says, 'in spite of the deadness of nature in Judea, there were special hidden forces.'[1]

The pool of Bethesda is one of these places where healing bubbles up even in the midst of death. Near the Sheep Gate, through which animals were led to sacrifice at the Temple, Jesus encounters the man who has been paralyzed for thirty-eight years.[2] He has been holding vigil in the place where hope has sprung up for many, though not yet for him. A weakness has taken hold of him, and even though he is close to the source of divine healing, he cannot access it.

The Judean setting serves as a symbol for the inner desert we all must enter if we are to become free, even if the experience leaves us weakened at first, and without external support. The man's loneliness also foreshadows the loneliness of Jesus, who will return to Jerusalem, be betrayed and abandoned by his friends, and led out alone through the Sheep Gate to Golgotha.

The fourth verse of this passage, which describes the angel who stirs up the waters and thus gives them their healing forces, is often omitted in modern translations because it does not appear in the earliest manuscripts. It seems unfortunate to lose this wonderful description, as without it, it is hard to understand why there is such a struggle for people to get into the pool at all. It is notable, however, that this particular man does not ever enter the water. Rather than being healed through contact with natural or angelic forces, he instead finds a new source of life springing up within him through his encounter with Christ.

In John, this healing is the second of only four that are described, whereas in Mark and Luke it is the fourth in the sequence (it is also described in Matthew, but at a later point). The first three healings in Mark and Luke show a progression from the inner to the outer sheaths of the human being: from the self displaced by demonic possession, through the soul inflamed with feverish emotion, to the damaged skin that should normally maintain the integrity of the body's life forces. Now, the illness of humanity has penetrated the entire physical organism: the body is paralyzed, unable to lift itself from the mineral realm upon which it rests.

In the Synoptic Gospels, sin and faith are mentioned here for the first time in connection with healing. Jesus tells the paralyzed man who has just been lowered down to him through the roof that his sins are forgiven. Somewhat surprisingly this is said not in response to the faith of the sick man himself, but to that of his friends who have gone to extreme measures to bring him to Jesus.

The word usually translated as 'sin' is *hamartia*, which literally means to miss the mark, such as when one aims an arrow at a target and does not hit it. *Hamartia* indicates an error, not an endemic quality of badness or wrongness. Human beings must be allowed to make mistakes, for that is the only way to learn in freedom. But the results of these mistakes, when they go too long uncorrected, can pile up, becoming a paralyzing burden.

Parts of our own souls may become stuck and frozen, just as certain members of a community can be paralyzed. The only way out is for the parts that are not so burdened and blocked to reach out in compassion, to believe in the potential of the frozen self and to bring it toward the place of healing, even if that requires effort or sacrifice. This faith, which turns toward a weaker element of the personality or the community to lift it up in love rather than castigating it with criticism and judgment, is what will gradually work through and release us from our 'sins', our piled-up errors. It is the same faith that God shows toward us and our ability to grow and learn, even though we are weak and fallible human creatures.

The man's subsequent identification of Jesus to the Pharisees has been interpreted by some as being malicious or at least misguided, but I think that is rather unfair. He has been filled with a great draught of truth and transparency that has restored clarity and uprightness to his physical body, and so he tells the truth when he is asked. Why should he not? Jesus did not tell him not to reveal his identity, and he appears undisturbed by the charges levelled against him that he has broken the Sabbath. Opposition is inevitable when our defense mechanisms are challenged, even when such opposition goes against our own best interests. True healers persist regardless of all the forces that rise against them.

In Jesus's time, something in the religious practice of the Israelites has lost its living power and has succumbed to the forces of the desert. Those who are bound up with the practices have a hard time admitting this, but Jesus has come to show a new way. Only human beings who change their hearts and minds (*metanoia*) and receive the baptism of Christ – an immersion not in water but in the spirit – will be able to see it. Only then can they rise from their bodily bed of death.

Human beings have to continually evolve, inwardly as well as outwardly, or else they fall into paralysis and death. The outer sheaths, of which any culturally given religion forms a part, must be enlivened from within, and that means being open to change and development while holding on to an intuitive knowledge of what is essential. What is at issue is how one practices and embodies one's faith, not whether any one person or any one faith is more perfect than another or has the right to exist. The spirit can enter many different earthly forms, but human beings must stay awake in order to keep the forms alive and re-create them if needed. This is as true for Christianity as for any other religion.

In all four Biblical accounts of this healing, the word *egeiro* is used, which means to 'cause to be raised up'. Now, however, the sufferer has the power to rise on his own when he heeds the divine call to life. But even when healed it is possible to fall back into error and darkness. In John's Gospel there is a second encounter in which Jesus warns the man who has been raised to uprightness, 'Sin no more.' As we will see in later healing stories, not just one but repeated meetings with the Healer are necessary in order to maintain our uprightness and keep mistakes from piling up again.

Personal Connections – Part 4

It was an ordinary Tuesday morning in the first week of a new school year in the eurythmy training. I was supposed to be graduating at the end of the year, but my successful completion was far from certain. While the teachers told me I had improved in the last few months, they weren't sure it would be enough for me to receive a diploma. I could try, but they were not very hopeful.

Five of my seven classmates had been told the same thing, although perhaps with a slightly more optimistic prognosis. This didn't make me feel any better; rather I was angry and frustrated at the way we were all treated. I didn't think we'd been listened to or properly understood.

That Tuesday morning our pianist, who lived in New Jersey, was late, and we were all standing around waiting and chatting together. When she finally appeared, wide-eyed with horror, she told us that a plane had crashed into the World Trade Center in Manhattan, thirty-five miles away.

It was September 11, 2001.

At first, I thought she meant it was an accident. A small plane had veered off course and somehow hit the building. But as classes came to a halt and we listened to the news, the reality became clear.

I was shocked by this dramatic expression of rage and violence, and with it striking so close to home I felt that the foundations of my world had been shaken. Something I had previously assumed to be inviolate was shown to be vulnerable. What would happen now? How would the United States respond? Would all-out war be unleashed?

'Homeland security' had always been an illusion, for nothing can ever be truly secure in our transitory world. The reaction to that illusion being unveiled, I suspected, was likely to be far worse than the attack that had provoked it. Human beings do not like it when the illusions that make us feel safe are taken away. Many will fight to the death to protect them. This doesn't make us any safer in reality, but fighting on behalf of reality requires another order of courage. It also requires knowing what is real and what isn't – which, as I had lately been finding out, is not easy to discern.

The school resumed its normal activities, but the shock touched us all. For days my view of the world was completely changed. As I looked around at people with whom I'd often been in conflict, including many of my classmates and teachers, the complaints and grievances that had so disturbed me no longer seemed to matter. All I wanted was the chance to be with people: to talk with them, work with them, engage with them, no matter how difficult it might be. Although soon my old patterns of thought and behavior returned, along with my usual grievances, I never forgot that extraordinary feeling of being briefly united with all humanity.

That fall, we were given time to process the attacks during a weekly all-school meeting. As I looked around the room I saw people from England, France, the Netherlands, Germany, Ukraine, Italy, and Japan, as well as from the United States and Canada. These were countries that in the time of our grandparents had been engaged in a bitter war, a war that must sometimes have seemed like the end of the world. Now we, their descendants, had come together through our training in a common spiritual striving. Surely that had to be worth something. It had to mean that progress was possible, that peace might one day come to Earth.

But there was still a lot of work to do, not least because peace did not reign in my own heart.

Before the attacks I had decided to formally join the Christian Community as a member. After a year of attending the services, I knew this was a path I could trust and could dedicate myself to. I hoped that such a commitment might help me cultivate the kind of inner strength I had been lacking. When I looked into myself, I saw that the same violent anger that drove a group of men to such a deadly attack also lived in me. If I didn't do as the terrorists did it was only because the circumstances of my life had been different. If I had been raised as they had been, with the same experiences and the same influences, then perhaps I would have acted in the same way. The underlying impulse was the same and was just as destructive.

It was my responsibility to overcome this urge, to quell this violence. Otherwise, who knew what harm might grow from it? Outwardly I might seem an innocuous and insignificant person, but my inner life did matter. It was a part of the whole realm of soul experience out of which outer deeds of violence proceed. My part might be very small, but it was the only thing I could do anything about.

This was why I stayed in the training, even when I seemed to be an utter failure, even when I felt so misunderstood by my well-meaning but unhelpful teachers. I'd started on this way as a path of healing, and I had to persevere for as long as I possibly could, even if healing seemed a distant and perhaps impossible goal. I should only leave the path if I had truly come to the end of it, and that had not happened yet. If I left something unfinished it would only grow and cause more harm in the future.

But the challenge was overwhelming. I needed help. I needed a refuge to contain me and keep me safe while I worked on that difficult task. In the sacraments I had finally found something that actually did help, that reduced my inflammability enough for me to take a first few steps forward, without having to damp myself down entirely, frozen and immobile.

I spoke to the priest about my decision, and would become a

member the following spring. In the midst of destruction, when so much lay in ruins, I could begin to build something. I could try to save my own soul, not only to benefit myself, but for the sake of a dying world.

Christ's question to the man at the pool, which can also be translated as 'Do you have the will to be healed?', was one that I had to hear as being addressed to me. Christ cannot heal me unless I also will it. And the truth is that none of us can be healed unless we are willing to admit that we are part of a larger whole, that we can't do it alone and need help. That also involves recognizing the terrible effect our continuing sickness and stubborn refusal to heal has on the structure of the whole, and thus recognizing the responsibility we bear for lifting up our own burden. If we don't, then the whole fabric of civilization is going to crumble, like a skyscraper sinking to the ground in a cloud of dust.

I was part of that fabric. I'd begun to work on my part. It was slow, and I was frequently discouraged and uncertain about my choices, but the way had begun to reveal itself. I had to pick up my bed, keep walking, and see where this way would lead me.

Meditation

Do you have the will to be healed?

5.
A Man with a Withered Hand:
Mark 3:1–6

On the Sabbath

The men of my family
have long served the Temple –
father to son, right back to the desert.
Yes, our line descends
from Kohath himself,
to whose sons were entrusted
the most holy things.

The ark, the menorah,
the table for bread,
the bread itself
that stood in the Presence.

The bread was our special service and care.
We baked it with reverence, guarding its secret,
we walked in procession to lay it down,

and to renew the offering.
On the Sabbath it was our privilege
to take and eat the food of God.

I say 'was', for I am a withered vine.
My line has ended in me. No son,
nor even a daughter blessed my house,
and my wife died lamenting her barrenness.
Not for her the joy of Sarah, of Hannah,
not for me the promise of Abraham.

When she breathed her last, I died as well.
I stumbled about, a mockery of a man,
seedless and sterile, an empty idol.
My service seemed so meaningless
I wasn't sorry it had to end.

Fruitless line, wasted life,
desert heart, withered hand –
it was all one, one sign of my deadness.
I came out here,
away from the Temple,
to live out my days
to their desolate end.

But here is where
I started to live.
Here I beheld
what makes a man.

How he dared – that one
in the synagogue –
to defy dead thoughts
and barren minds.

On the Sabbath, their thoughts were of emptiness.
They'd come to an end, and didn't know it.

He showed me the way
that leads past the end.
He told me to stand
and to stretch, he dared me
to live, not to lie
like bread on a table,
helplessly waiting
to be consumed.

He gave me himself,
and I took, and ate.

Reflections on *A Man with a Withered Hand*

When I tried to imagine what profession the man with the withered hand could have belonged to, what work he might have done with his hands, I pictured him serving the Temple. This meant that his handicap was not merely personal but the sign of a malaise affecting his whole people.

The priesthood of the Jerusalem Temple was a hereditary position: priests traced their line back to Aaron, the brother of Moses, and all belonged to the tribe of Levi just as Aaron and Moses did. The entire tribe was dedicated to religious service, and the Torah lays out in detail their sacred tasks as well as how they are to be supported in their duty by the rest of the community.

In Numbers 3:11–13, the Lord tells Moses that he is consecrating the tribe of Levi to himself. The entire tribe takes the place of the first male offspring of every Israelite woman, who would otherwise belong to the Lord because he saved their lives when he destroyed the firstborn in Egypt – the event commemorated by Passover. This hereditary priestly service is thus of supreme importance and has great symbolic meaning. It is not just a logistical convenience. When a priest's line failed, therefore, when there was no son to carry on the tradition, I imagined that it must have been a matter of tremendous concern and heartache, even of existential dread. If the tribe of Levi died out, then the people of Israel could face death as well, the same death that had passed them over when they were brought out of slavery in Egypt.

There were three groups of Levites, named after the three sons of Levi: Kohath, Gershon and Merari. I made my speaker in the poem a Kohathite, a member of the group of priests who were tasked with handling and caring for the holy objects of the Temple, including the bread that was placed in the presence of the divinity and had to be constantly replenished. The duties of the Kohathites are detailed in Chapter 4 of Numbers. During the period when there was no temple, just a portable tabernacle being transported through the desert, they were to carry the most sacred items, but only after these holy objects had been covered by Aaron and his sons, lest those lower in the priestly hierarchy be struck by death (Numbers 4:15). Being close to the divine presence is dangerous for the unprepared. All the rules and regulations of the ancient Israelites are directed toward this goal: cultivating a new relationship between human beings and the divine, under conditions that protect the fragile, vulnerable human core.

But by the time of Jesus, something had gone awry. The Temple itself had been desecrated and destroyed by conquering forces, and although it was subsequently rebuilt and the order of worship re-established, there must have been much unease around that practice. Under Roman rule the descendants of Israel were no longer sovereign over the land they believed had been promised to them by God. They were subject to yet another invading force that could revoke their religious rights at a whim. Their safety was precarious, their future uncertain. Were their sacrifices even still valid and effective? Where was the God who had promised to protect them?

All of this came together for me in the character of a man whose noble priestly power has fallen away from him, has withered and become impotent. Significantly, this is the first of the healings in the Synoptic Gospels in which healing on the Sabbath is made an issue by the scribes and Pharisees, although Jesus has healed on the Sabbath before without anyone objecting. (In the Gospel of John, the objections begin already with the invalid by the pool of Bethesda, as we have seen.) This, too, seems to point to the healing of the man's withered hand as a comment upon the mission of Israel as a whole. It disturbs those authorities who have become invested in maintaining the status quo or in shaping it according to their own ideas of how it should be. They resist seeing that a radically new approach is needed.

This healing directly follows the story of Jesus and his disciples plucking heads of grain on the Sabbath and being rebuked by the Pharisees, to which Jesus responds: 'The Sabbath was made for man, not man for the Sabbath. So the Son of Man is Lord even of the Sabbath' (Mark 2:27–28). A new concept of worship is needed, one that does not chain human beings to fixed ideas but is inwardly alive and able to transform them.

Whereas when he healed the leper, Jesus stretched out his hand to touch him, now he asks this man to stretch out his own hand. In order to achieve the healing and restoration of one's mission in the world, one has to become inwardly active. In a sense Jesus did not heal the man; rather, the man healed himself by responding to the call to do something impossible. How could he stretch his cramped, incapacitated, withered hand? Yet he dared to reach out to an unknown future.

The idea of human faith as a healing power, which first arose with the man by the pool in the previous chapter, is strengthened and individualized. This theme will continue to develop throughout the entire sequence of healings.

Personal Connections – Part 5

A few years after 9/11, my life had changed. I had graduated from the eurythmy school in what I had come to think of as a 'thirteenth-hour miracle' because the teachers had let our class go through the whole graduation process – including the final performance – and only then decided to grant us our diplomas.

Not only had I graduated, I'd even gotten married. My husband, Michael, was a fellow eurythmist, a decade older than me, who had grown up and studied in Switzerland. He was now a eurythmy therapist and part of the performing stage group connected with the eurythmy school. He had been my neighbor in campus housing for a year when he suddenly declared that he loved me and wanted to marry me.

'I want to have a family with you,' he said, confessing that he'd never felt this way before.

Michael was a teacher, a healer, and an artist – all the things I admired but thought myself incapable of becoming. With this marriage I believed I would be able to ride along on his healing energy. His affection and appreciation had certainly boosted me through my last, grueling semester in eurythmy school. He made me feel special and gave me a purpose: to help and support his life-giving impulse.

My wish to 'be with people' had been granted. At last, I was in an intimate relationship, proving that I was capable of love and worthy of love after all.

But all was not well under the surface. I had not listened to my body, which still did not feel ready to enter into an intimate physical union. I had forced it to go forward, ignoring its protests, its continued numbness and lack of desire. Still, at least I didn't experience the horrible out-of-body inner split that I had on previous occasions, and I did feel safe and cared for by Michael in many ways. Maybe this was the best chance I was ever going to get, I thought.

And so I went into marriage like a sleepwalker. I didn't fully understand that I was binding myself on subtle levels to another person, someone I barely knew, without being completely open with him and without appreciating that he might be bearing hidden wounds of his own. It was a marriage in which our shadow sides, still unpenetrated, loomed large, waiting to ambush us.

At the time, I was working for the eurythmy school and stage group. They had asked me if I would do publicity and advertising and, in need of a job, I had said yes. I also wanted to support eurythmy and the teachers, who, I thought, now accepted and appreciated me following my graduation miracle. One of the projects I had to work on was a large, ambitious tour to perform Dvořák's *New World Symphony*. Eurythmists were being auditioned to join the expanded group.

The audition took the form of a workshop and was scheduled for later in the summer after Michael and I were married. We were both involved in the workshop. As a longtime member of the stage group, Michael had participated in developing the choreography for the piece. But he wouldn't be part of the tour; he was leaving the stage group now that he was married to me and could get a green card, and he was due to start a new, full-time job as a eurythmy therapist at the local Waldorf school.

As for me, I was thrilled by the prospect of being part of such an exciting project. It didn't occur to me that I might not pass the audition. Surely everyone local would be taken on first, with a few extras to supplement them, I assumed. My grandiose feelings resurfaced, and I could see no reason why I should not be chosen.

Some weeks later, I went into the office at the school to pick up my mail. In my box was an official envelope from the stage group director. I opened it eagerly in front of the secretary, who must have seen my jaw drop and my face freeze in astonished dismay. The letter was a form response telling me that I had not been chosen for the project, but thanking me for auditioning, signed: one of my former teachers.

It was a perfectly polite and objectively reasonable letter, but it aroused in me a devastating sense of rejection. My worth as a person was suddenly called into question again.

Worse still, my job involved doing publicity for the symphony project and I would have to continue with it. Also, I was part of a secondary stage group from which everyone else had been accepted into the project. When they went to practice for the symphony, I alone had to pack up my things and go home.

Nobody talked to me about how I was feeling or acknowledged that it might be hard for me. I had received the same letter as everyone else who had not been chosen, which was fair of course. Except that I didn't think I was like everyone else. No one else was working on the project and so had to face their failure every day. Others who were not chosen could recover in privacy. I couldn't. To me it was a public, humiliating rejection, and the silence made it more humiliating still.

I was crushed by all the negative feelings I thought I had overcome: envy, hurt, pride, anger, depression.

Why didn't I go to the director and talk to her about it? I knew I would only break down and cry. I would not be able to say anything. And if I did, I would only be looked down upon as unable to handle rejection like a grown-up, a professional. My failure would be confirmed and compounded. So I continued in silence, again.

The devastation I felt was greater than the circumstances warranted. After all, no one wanted to hurt me. The real problem was that I had once more been forced to confront my own illusions about myself. My constant fear of exclusion, of being cast out of human society due to my failures and weaknesses, had been activated. Despite my occasional prideful feelings about myself as a performer, I knew that this was the real issue: not being judged and found wanting as an individual artist, but being excluded from the social group. It triggered an existential dread in me, a fear that was really about death. It was as if I had been killed and cast out into the outer darkness with cold indifference.

My strategy for dealing with the situation was not effective. I wanted to appear strong and conceal my emotional vulnerability, but when people treated me as if I really was strong, I got upset. I wanted them to see the real me, even as I worked very hard to prevent them from doing so. I was expecting too much of them. In our Western culture, we are encouraged to keep a critical distance from others as a protective measure, and as a result are frequently unaware of the pain we cause. People could not feel what I was feeling, and if I didn't speak up, they had no way of knowing what was going on inside me.

At the time, I had no such insights to comfort me. I only knew that every day at work, every time I was handed a task in support of the symphony, every time my colleagues looked at me with unspoken pity in their eyes or maybe contempt, my composure was shattered and my rage threatened to burst out with destructive force. The only way I knew for handling this was to suppress it.

That also meant cutting off relationships and withdrawing from situations I found difficult. I quit my job at the eurythmy school and took a teaching position in a nearby Waldorf school. I had little confidence in my ability as a teacher, but I had to get away from the pain somehow.

This episode reminded me of something that happened to me when I was in high school. I had gone inner-tubing at a ski slope with a group of friends and came home with frostbite. Too much snow had lodged between my glove and the cuff of my jacket, and it had frozen my wrist. I couldn't move my right hand, which was also my writing hand. I was terrified. Would I ever be able to move it again? What would happen to me? I mustn't let anybody find out. I struggled to do my schoolwork with my left hand. I was glad that I played the violin in orchestra, so that my right hand only had to move the bow while my left did the tricky fingering. I confided my fears only to my diary, letting my left hand shakily scribble what my mouth refused to speak.

After a few days, the numbness went away. But the coldness in my soul was not gone. Why was I unable to tell anyone what had happened? I hadn't done anything bad; I wasn't at fault for incurring a physical injury. Why did I feel I had to conceal myself from everyone? Why was I so desperately afraid of doing something wrong and being cast out of the kingdom?

The same question arose in me with my rejection from the symphony project. Like a withered hand, my creative will had somehow become numb and dead. Underneath that numbness lay a suppressed fire, a frustrated longing for self-expression and meaningful work. Despite repeated failures, I didn't give up. I kept trying to find my way in the world, to find the work that I could do and the people who would accept me. Nudged by the Healer who was accompanying me unseen, I would keep on stretching myself, reaching out for the impossible.

The trouble was that I tended to stretch myself too far, too fast, refusing to admit my weakness and incapacity, and this only led to more humiliating failures. My prideful habit of concealment had to be broken down before real healing could happen. The Pharisee in me would have to step back and acknowledge the Lord of the Sabbath.

Meditation

Stretch out your hand.

6.
A Centurion's Servant:
Luke 7:1–10

The Commander's Word

They called me his servant, and so I was,
from the hour of my birth, got of a slave
in my master's house. No one said 'son',
but they knew – his wife was barren,
while my face mirrored his and told the tale.

He loved my mother, though he could not wed her,
loved me, although I couldn't enter
the army he also loved and served.

The best he could do was to let me serve him,
to follow him everywhere, bearing his armor,
guarding him as he guarded the Empire.

He even brought me into the Temple,
the dark and hidden chamber

below the earth, where the bull of Heaven
is killed to bring us life.

There I became a servant of Mithras,
enduring all trials for my father's sake –
he would have me a warrior of the spirit,
if not a soldier of Rome.

Then he was called to Palestine.
He brought me, of course – said farewell to my mother,
and sailed with the legion to keep the peace.

After many adventures, we washed up here,
in a fisherman's town by the inland sea,
among the Jews. They worship not
bull-slayers in caves, but a god whose name
they carry unspoken, so holy they hold him,
a god whose first command was light.
Each seventh day they stop to rest,
and do no work, saying their god
commanded them so. A strange command,
and yet it drew me, bound as I was
to the restless will of Rome.

My master saw it, and cared for the people
in part for my sake – himself not called
by a shapeless Word, he honored my quest.
Yet how could I fulfil it?
I was no Jew, nor truly Roman;
I had no place in this world.

Whenever my master – my father – died
I'd be unmoored, adrift in a chaos
where no god spoke me to life.

There was a teacher among the Jews,
who came at times to our town
amidst rumors of healings and wonders.
He even broke their Sabbath
to bring men relief – but not for me.
I did not keep their rest,
and could not share their salvation.

But one day I fell ill. My body knew
how to keep Sabbath, if I did not.
It confined me to bed and stopped my work.
My master was worried, then alarmed.
This illness carried me close to death,
and indeed, without the longed-for Word
I had no wish to live.

My master heard the Teacher was passing.
He sent him word of his need, begging help.
My death would grieve him greatly.

The Jews repaid his kindness in kind.
They'd bring their treasure to our foreign home.
But my master stopped them. 'No,' he said,
'his word is enough. It's what my boy needs.
I am a commander of human bodies,
but he the commander of souls.

Let the boy
join *his* army.'

So my master released me,
my father gave birth,
and a word
became life.

Reflections on *A Centurion's Servant*

This healing does not appear in Mark. In Luke, it is placed after the healing of the man with the withered hand, and after Jesus has called the twelve apostles and given a number of teachings (the 'Sermon on the Plain'). In Matthew, it immediately follows the healing of the leper, which, as we have seen, follows the Sermon on the Mount given to the disciples as a basis for their work. This healing is therefore connected to apostleship and to the widening of the mission of Israel to a greater body of humanity. The promise given to Abraham – that his descendants would become a blessing for the whole world (Genesis 12:3) – is to be fulfilled.

Abraham obeyed the command of the Lord to leave his homeland and go to another place so that this promised blessing could come to pass. At the time, he was already old, had no legitimate son and therefore no descendants, and no way of seeing how such a thing could be possible. Nevertheless, he trusted in the divine promise. When the Lord told him his descendants would be as numerous as the stars, 'he believed the Lord, and he counted it to him as righteousness' (Genesis 15:6).

Long before the establishment of the Temple and its system of sacrifices and laws, what mattered was that a relationship of trust should exist between God and humanity. Abraham did not need to follow a long list of commandments in order to be counted as righteous, he merely had to trust in the promise of God and go where he was told to go. Not because he feared what would happen if he didn't, but because something wondrously good was in store if he did.

By the time of Jesus, this intimate, trusting relationship had been lost, replaced by the fear of putting a foot wrong and being punished for it. Even a military official from a foreign invading force might have a better sense of this original relationship than many Jews: he would know what power there can be in the living word, in the powerful command that directs armies and changes lives.

The official in Matthew and Luke is called a 'centurion' and we are told he is based in Capernaum. One might assume that he was a member of a Roman legion, but there were no Roman forces in Galilee at this time. Most likely the soldier would have belonged to the forces of Herod Antipas, a client king of Rome.[1] Capernaum itself, site of many of the early healings, was located beside the ancient Via Maris, a route along which trade caravans and military forces moved between the great powers of Mesopotamia and Egypt. When Jesus left Nazareth in the Galilean heights, site of a community of the ascetic Essenes, to make his center of activity in Capernaum, it indicated a move toward the life of the great world, a place from which movement was possible in many directions.[2]

When describing Jesus's move from Nazareth to Capernaum, Matthew quotes Isaiah: 'The people dwelling in darkness have seen a great light, and for those dwelling in the region and shadow of death, on them a light has dawned' (Matthew 4:16; compare with Isaiah 9:2). The implication is that light is to be brought to the 'peoples' outside of the Israelite community, who have not yet received the blessing of Abraham's covenant. With the healing of the centurion's servant in Capernaum, this mission is put into story form.

In my telling, I have given the soldier a Roman origin and left his exact career trajectory vague. This is less important than his foreignness. Matthew emphasizes that the centurion's faith outdoes that of the 'sons of the kingdom', the actual descendants of Abraham, who will 'be thrown into the outer darkness' for their lack of just this essential quality. Luke omits these harsh words, instead praising the soldier's love for the Jewish people, which even extended to building a synagogue for them. This inspired me to wonder how a foreigner might engage with the Jewish faith and what an encounter with their Messiah could mean to him.

The Persian cult of Mithras was adopted by Roman soldiers and spread throughout the Empire in the first century AD, forming a serious rival to Christianity in its early years. An all-male religion, it was practiced in underground sanctuaries, or Mithraea, where the central ritual of bull sacrifice was performed. In surviving images of Mithras subduing the bull, we can see how this divine helper was imagined as a model and guide for humans struggling to overcome the forces of their own lower nature. Mithras looks straight out at the viewer, not down at the bull, as is also seen in images of St. Michael conquering the dragon. Sometimes he looks up to the sun god, Helios, showing that, as Bastiaan Baan explains, even such a 'powerful being from the angelic hierarchies does not fight subhuman nature on his own, but needs support from higher forces.'[3]

The Roman soldier and servant of my poem come to recognize and acknowledge a higher authority than Mithras. They see in Christ Jesus the supreme power who, if we focus our gaze on him, can help us achieve a right relationship to all that threatens us from the depths of our own being. Such a recognition is a necessity for all who would make the transition from the old, pre-Christian mysteries to the new.

A variant of this story is found in the Gospel of John. There, among other differences, the 'official' is not identified as Roman, and the suffering ill person is his son rather than his servant. This led me to imagine one way that the boy could be at the same time a 'servant' and a 'son'. The word translated as 'servant' in Matthew and Luke is *paîs*, which can also mean child or young man.

In either case, the faith of someone other than the ill person is what moves Jesus and enables healing power to flow through him toward the sufferer. Our relationships, our bonds of loving care, which exist within and outside family ties of blood, are potential carriers of healing. And yet, close and loving as we may be, respect for individual freedom is necessary for the healing to be effective.

The divine Word is a creative force that can only be heard privately, in the innermost sanctum of our soul. And there, it has a power that goes beyond even the physical presence or touch of Jesus the healer: a generative, transformative quality that restores what is most truly human in us.

Personal Connections – Part 6

Teaching children proved to be far too difficult for me in my emotionally frozen, wounded state. But before many months had passed I became pregnant and had an excuse to stop. This escape wasn't consciously intentional, but the pregnancy removed me from a situation that I couldn't openly admit was too much for me. Little did I know it would plunge me into a far more challenging job from which there could be no exit.

The birth was quick and without complications: a planned home birth that left me exhausted but exhilarated and happy with our beautiful boy, Brendan. The trouble began when he had difficulty nursing. I first became aware of this through the pain it caused me, the gnawing, burning sensation in my nipples that made every feeding an agony. I got some advice to get him into a better position and that helped my discomfort, but not his milk intake.

I didn't realize at first. Or rather, I did realize, but with my capacity for denial, I made myself ignore it. I knew the small size of the yellowish spots on his diapers indicated he was not getting enough liquid, but I told myself they were wet enough. I wanted to avoid yet more scrutiny and intervention.

Why did I do this? Why did I endanger a baby's life with my coldness and indifference?

I was already suffering – from the pain in my breasts, the turmoil and disruption of our regular life, and especially the disruption to my sleep. A hungry baby is hard to soothe. He screamed inconsolably, and I felt helpless and incompetent as well as exhausted. As always, I dealt with my helplessness by hiding it and pretending that it wasn't there.

It was a self-protective gesture, an outgrowth of lifelong habits that had left me inwardly starved for emotional nourishment myself. A mother's selfless instinct to protect her child in preference to her own life depends upon her being healthy and strong, at least in certain ways. It doesn't come out of nowhere, and if it's not there it doesn't mean the mother is a monster. It means that somewhere in her, she still carries a version of herself as an un-nourished infant. This inner infant will be her first priority in a crisis of survival.

One infant cannot nourish another, however; we have to grow up first. But I didn't know that then, and I did not have an opportunity to discover it at the time. This was a daily emergency.

There was more: under such stressful circumstances, Michael had changed. He was no longer caring and nurturing of me. Instead he became angry and critical, blaming me for not being able to take care of everything. He huddled in a corner and said, 'I don't want this!'

What happened to 'I want to have family with you'? That had been a passing fancy, it seemed. He *didn't* want children, he said now, not if it was going to cause chaos and disruption and extra work for him.

Michael had been fooled by my mask of competence. I didn't set out to deceive him, and I thought he knew me better than that, but it turned out he didn't. When my weakness was revealed to him, he was terrified, and turned to self-protective measures. He, too, was bearing an un-nourished infant within him, which I had never seen before. And I still didn't understand what I was seeing in this moment of crisis; I was only shocked by the loss of a supportive partner I thought I could depend upon.

He didn't show this side when other people were around, and I didn't think anyone would believe me if I told them. He was famous in our community for being caring: a compassionate healer whom everyone adored.

It must be all my fault, I thought. Maybe I was not loving enough.

That was very likely, given my history. And I was having a hard time loving the baby, for sure. But I couldn't tell anyone about that either. I was too ashamed, too afraid of judgment and criticism.

Brendan's lack of milk intake was discovered in spite of me when the midwife weighed him. He wasn't sucking well enough, and wasn't gaining weight. I had to pump milk, but pumps are not as effective as a real baby, and it wasn't enough. We supplemented with donated breast milk that my midwife helped us find in the community, and with formula. I kept going with the pumping for eight months before finally giving up.

Brendan survived, but I felt like a failure at a mother's main task: feeding my child. Instead of a pleasant, natural bonding experience, it was a chaos of expensive machines and foreign devices and worry that there wouldn't be enough. I had to put Brendan down when I pumped, which was several times a day, breaking our connection instead of strengthening it as the milk was produced. People gave me all kinds of conflicting advice that left me even more confused, and no one could ever explain what was causing the problem. The closest anyone came was saying that he had a very high palate which might make it difficult for him to take in the nipple far enough.

As further cause for dismay, Brendan didn't lift his head or roll over on schedule, and he was diagnosed as developmentally delayed. There was more alarm from the experts and more calls for intervention. Therapists came and worked with him, with no noticeable effect. I felt again that if something was wrong with him, there must be something wrong with me. He came out of me, after all.

And I couldn't love him. I felt responsibility for him, but not love. Sometimes his unmet, insatiable needs made me so angry that I had to put him down and go to another room to scream or hit things, which scared and alienated Michael further. He told me that *I* should get help, pronouncing judgment upon me, but not admitting he might be involved in any way.

I didn't get help. I didn't tell anyone. I felt sure that I was a terrible person for not being an instantly loving and caring mother.

At one point I wished I had never met Michael, so that none of this would have happened. Then I thought, 'But I couldn't wish Brendan not to exist.'

That was a turning point. I couldn't feel love for him, I didn't have wonderful, gooey, pleasurable feelings of delight in connection with him, but I did want him to exist. If it was my task to support that, I would do it.

I now know that this *is* love. Love means creating and holding a space where another person can exist, independent of you and of any influence they may have upon you, positive or negative, simply because each human ego has a right to existence. It doesn't necessarily mean warm fuzzy feelings of connection and pleasure. Those usually do come along with parenthood, and thankfully so, but their absence doesn't mean a more fundamental kind of love can't be present.

At the time, I didn't know this. I couldn't think very clearly. I only knew I had to go on with a task I wasn't sure I could complete, yet that was indelibly mine.

Things slowly got easier. I learned ways to manage the feeding and to soothe Brendan and get more sleep. Michael thawed out and became more affectionate again; he loved Brendan and stopped saying he didn't want him. I welcomed this, desperate for the connection and validation for which I depended on Michael, but I didn't feel fully comfortable or safe with him after that. I would always be scared of the cold, dark hardness underneath the warmth, which occasionally jumped out and hurt me again. But I divided this awareness from everyday life and tried not to think about it.

As Brendan grew, I did come to feel affection and love for him; he was undeniably adorable, and I began to enjoy him in a 'normal' way. As I became more competent with the everyday challenges of baby care, my feelings of inadequacy and self-loathing diminished. But I still felt an underlying insecurity with Brendan, as well as with Michael. He seemed to like Michael more than me, and was easier and less fussy with him. Unsure of our connection, I held back inwardly. I was not aware of how sensitive a baby's mirroring instinct is, so that even the most subtle inner hesitation in me would cause him to also hold back, making me worry that he 'didn't like me'.

In this way, the old dance of withdrawal and non-responsiveness I'd been doing all my life continued. A distance opened up, not a full estrangement, but a gap, an empty space that was filled with uncertainty, anxiety, lack of information. Brendan and I grew together, and apart. I was unable to stop judging myself in our relationship, and condemning myself as a failure. I could not see that this wasn't all about me, but about another person with his own independent reality. And so we could never truly meet.

At the same time, I was moved and humbled by the bravery of this small person who had come to me, in spite of all my weakness and handicaps. In complete helplessness, he had entrusted himself to me. I wasn't worthy of such trust, but I would keep trying anyway.

Brendan's first tooth came in at seven months, and very soon after that he rolled over. From then on, his motor skills developed steadily. We let the therapists go. At fourteen months he was walking. What I remember from his first steps is how he would laugh every time he fell down. For him, failure was not a stroke of doom, but a hilarious joke. And then he would get up and try again.

This was the lesson he had come to teach me, the divine Word he wanted to impress upon my heart, but I was still having a very hard time hearing the message from the angels. I had to learn not to be terrified of failure, of the death of my limited, restrictive lower ego that kept me bound to old ways of being. Only once I learned to make that sacrifice could my inner child be healed.

> *Meditation*
>
> Lord, I am not worthy to have you come under my roof, but only say the word and my child will be healed.

7.
The Young Man of Nain:
Luke 7:11–17

Son of the Widow

I never saw my father's face.
He died far away, lost in some war
before my birth, and left us two
alone in the battle of life.
I did my duty, my mother's love
repaid by efforts no one could fault.
My own love, though, lay elsewhere:
my heart's desire to go behind
the mask of matter that hides the truth,
and open its secrets to all.

What drove me was the wish to know
how things work, what makes them run,
the mysteries of life and motion.
The heartbeat of a frightened bird.
held in my two cupped hands,

the wheeling stars that far above
mark earthly times and seasons –
What binds them together, what connects
each thing to every other?
To leave it to God was not enough.
My own mind must divine the answers,
lifting the veil of nature to reveal
reality itself.

And so I worked – by day in the fields,
toiling for bread to feed myself
and my poor widowed mother;
by night, a snatch of sleep, then up
before the sun to search for light,
pushing my mind to lengths no man
had ever reached before.
I sought, I saw, I knew – I fell
before the face of God.

So they found me, took me for dead,
and laid me out for burial.
My mother wailed once, then was dumb.
She walked by the bier in her widow's veil,
dark as the barren earth.

And as they bore me toward the gate
I knew my spirit could not bear
another crossing. At that threshold
my flickering spark would be snuffed out
and night would fall at last.

That's where he met us – his crowd facing mine,
streaming behind us like the trails
of two opposing arrows.
I sought to leave the earth; he came
to meet it, fill it, know it all,
with wisdom born of love.

He looked not at me, but at my mother;
her plight moved him, not mine.
I had transgressed, and justice said
that I must pay the price.

But she had not sinned. Should she be bereft
of her only care and support?
Should even my reluctant, grudging aid
be denied her innocent heart?

Should the earth be deprived
of my feeble life
because I longed for death?

He did not ask these questions, and yet
they shot into me like arrows.
Lying there, helpless,
as if I were dead,
I saw how I'd never lived.

If he told me to stand
and face life on earth,
I'd do it now.
Not to seek to see God,
but to be a man,
if he would show the way.

His hand has stilled
my fleeing soul,
and I await his summons.
Oh Mother, forgive me.
I've so much to tell
your patient, listening heart.
I won't leave you alone again.

Reflections on The Young Man of Nain

The raising from death of the young man of Nain is the first of four healings described only in the Gospel of Luke. Rudolf Steiner connects this story with a legend, related in Schiller's poem 'The Veiled Statue of Saïs', which tells of a youth who profaned the Egyptian mysteries when he tore the veil from the statue of Isis and was punished by death.

In the Egyptian mysteries, a candidate for initiation was called 'Son of the Widow'. The central myth underlying this initiatory process was that of Isis, Osiris and Horus: Osiris, the husband of Isis, is killed and dismembered by the forces of evil, but he is reborn through her as Horus, the divine son. The veil of Isis represents the world of the senses that obscures our vision of the spiritual world. As long as our knowledge and perception are dependent upon the physical senses, we lose all awareness of the world beyond until the moment of death, when the veil is lifted. This is why, according to Plutarch, the phrase 'No mortal has ever lifted my veil' was written above the statue of Isis at Saïs. One who deliberately cultivates the power to lift this veil and see behind the sense-perceptible world is an initiate, a son of Isis: a Son of the Widow.

Rudolf Steiner said that in our time, humanity as a whole is undergoing initiation.[1] But this is a perilous undertaking. Initiation leads to increased power, which demands greater responsibility and an awareness of the damage that can be caused by our impatience, greed and egotism. Much damage has already been done: from the creation of the atomic bomb to genetic engineering to climate change, these are all results of untrammelled human manipulation of the forces of nature. And yet it is not possible to put the veil back. We can only try to find a way into the future, in spite of all the obstacles that we have created. Unless we can change ourselves and find the new way forward, we will be struck down by the forces of death.

Materialistic, intellectual thinking cannot save us from the perils that face us now. As Gus Speth, a US advisor on climate change, has said:

> I used to think that the top environmental problems were biodiversity loss, ecosystem collapse and climate change. I thought that thirty years of good science could address these problems. I was wrong. The top environmental problems are selfishness, greed and apathy, and to deal with these we need a cultural and spiritual transformation. And we scientists don't know how to do that.[2]

The need for transformation was already present at the time of Jesus. Up until then, the focus had been on developing the element within the human being that was capable of creating a free, independent relationship with its divine origins: the human ego. But in order to be free, this ego had to be cut off from the divine world and lose all awareness of its true nature. It had to be capable of error, of untrue thinking, of immoral action. It had to be vulnerable to death, not merely as a release from physical existence, but as an end point beyond which no further growth was possible.

This created an impasse, for such a death-bearing, disconnected ego could not, out of its own forces, lift itself up and return to life again. Another impulse had to be brought in, a breath of life from the divine world that could revive the dead child of the human line.

This picture is given to us in the raising of the young man of Nain. His dead body is being carried over the threshold of the gates of the city, out of the realm of life, attended by a large crowd. Jesus meets this crowd with his own entourage, moving in the opposite direction, into the earthly world. Notably, he is moved by compassion, not for the dead man, but for his mother. Our earth, that motherly sheath that bears us through life, will itself die unless we, her wayward children, can raise ourselves to a new level of insight and responsibility.

But there is hope. Christ approaches from the divine world and brings the possibility for life to spring anew. In the story, the touch of Jesus halts the man's forward motion toward the grave. A moment of stillness, a free space in which the human being can potentially activate its living forces, is created. Jesus speaks to the dead man, again, as with the paralyzed man, telling him to 'arise' (*egeiro*). But he now prefaces this with, 'Young man, I say to you…' (Luke 7:14), which would seem unnecessary from a logical point of view: it is quite obvious that he is speaking and to whom. However, these words, drawn from the ancient mysteries, are important in establishing a new relationship between the creative forces of nature and the immobile human offspring. Whereas in the healing of the centurion's servant that immediately preceded this encounter, Christ's word alone was able to work without his personal presence, he now adds his personal essence, his 'I', to the process. The man awakes through finding himself in personal relationship with Christ, and he can in turn now speak.

Speech is the supreme creative activity of the Hebrew God, who spoke the world into existence in the first chapter of Genesis. When human beings who have faced the perils of death come back to life and begin to speak, they are able to bring something of that creative spirit into the mortal world. Reunited with their mother, they will sustain and support her, as she once was supported by the fatherly ground of existence. Connection has been restored; life can go on.

Personal Connections – Part 7

When Brendan was two years old, I got pregnant again.

We weren't exactly trying for another baby, but we weren't *not* trying. Michael thought it would be good for Brendan to have a sibling. 'But you'll have to do all the extra work,' he told me, in complete seriousness.

I nodded and smiled, but inside I was screaming. I didn't want another child when I didn't even feel comfortable with the first one. I couldn't bear to lose Michael's affection and support again, to go back into that black hole of loveless despair.

I blamed myself for being deficient. My sense of being in the wrong was reinforced by the fact that whenever we had an argument or I was upset with Michael, he would never apologize or admit to any fault. He gave me the silent treatment until I backed down and said I was sorry. In some ways this was attractive because it offered me a strange kind of agency: if I was the bad one, then I could make myself better.

A lot of Michael's anger was about the messiness of our house. It didn't disturb me, but from time to time he got angry and told me how much it annoyed him. I would make some small effort to pick up or clean, and would feel like I was doing a lot, but it was never enough for him. I simply didn't notice the mess, just as I hadn't noticed the brown toilet back in Seattle. I didn't want to be annoying, but it was hard for me to unlearn old ways and see more fully what was around me. Since messiness didn't bother me, it was easy to slip back into it until it provoked another outburst.

Neither did Michael confide in me much about his own inner life. I didn't understand that he felt trapped in a job he didn't enjoy because he had to support us. I only knew that he was angry and resentful when I wanted to go out or have time for myself. As far as he was concerned it meant I was not doing my job, which was to care for the family and the house. He said my problem was that I was a 'modern woman' who wanted help with the housework, but he was not a modern man. This was all new to me! We had always shared the housework and he had never complained. But having a baby changed things.

I felt weighed down in my turn by the drudgery of housework and looking after the baby. I didn't have time or energy for anything other than serving the baby's insatiable needs. Just before Brendan's birth, I had sold a couple of essays to national magazines, and I had hoped to do more writing. But inspiration had fled. I even stopped writing in a journal after a while. My honest thoughts were dark and depressing, and when I recorded my 'everything is fine' thoughts, they felt false and unreal. I dimly sensed everything that I was pressing down into my unconscious, but I wasn't ready to bring it up into the light. The result was that my creative energy was lost. I assumed I was too lazy, too lacking in perseverance, or maybe just lacking some inner fire needed to create art. I ought to give up and focus on family life.

When I missed my period, I went to my midwife to confirm the news, pretending I was happy about the possibility of being pregnant again. She listened to my abdomen, but when she couldn't find a heartbeat she sent me to have an ultrasound.

The technician was uncommunicative, speaking only to instruct me to get up on the table. She moved her probe around on my stomach for a very long time, peering at her monitor with her head on one side, then the other. Then she told me to get down and that I'd be sent the results. I couldn't tell anything from her demeanor.

All I could think as I lay there on that cold, hard table, in a dim, silent room, was how relieved I would be if this pregnancy quietly went away.

How could I be hoping for a miscarriage? How uncaring, how selfish I was. I must really be a monster, I thought.

The results came in. The baby was not alive.

Because it was early on in the pregnancy, we hadn't told anyone, so it was only with Michael that I had to pretend to be sad. He hugged me and reassured me we could try again, while inwardly I screamed, '*No!*'

I was given the choice of either having the foetal tissue removed or waiting until I miscarried naturally. I chose to wait. It took several weeks of slow bleeding and anxious wondering.

Finally, I said something to Michael about my reluctance to have more children. I still couldn't tell him the whole story about how his reaction to Brendan's birth had affected me, but I admitted that I didn't fully share his wish for another child. He was able to accept that. The next evening, while he was out, I had powerful, painful cramps that sent me to the toilet. Groaning, I passed a clump of blood and tissue that I immediately flushed away.

I suddenly felt released and full of new energy. Things would be different now, maybe.

The thoughts and feelings I'd striven to hide from myself were pushed even farther away. I was immersed in life and work and childcare, trying to be a good enough mother, a good enough wife. The bad times with Michael didn't come frequently, and when they did, I waited them out.

In spite of Michael's grumbling, I had carved out some time to do a couple of part-time jobs; he couldn't deny that we needed the money. I enjoyed my work in editing, graphic design, and publicity, which gave me a creative and social outlet. There were people who appreciated my work, who valued what I did and didn't complain that it wasn't enough. That gave me the confidence to try new things.

I was also getting better at cooking and enjoyed that, too. As with cleaning, I'd never learned to cook. After leaving college, where meals were provided, I'd survived largely on canned soup and pasta mixed with sauce from a jar. Now, I signed up to receive vegetable deliveries from a local farm, and studied cookbooks for ideas on how to use unfamiliar vegetables like celeriac and mizuna. I made a Thanksgiving turkey with all the trimmings. I pored over research on the benefits of lacto-fermented foods and made sauerkraut and yogurt. I learned how to bake sourdough bread and began baking every week. I even taught a few bread-baking workshops, venturing into teaching again for the first time since my last disastrous experience. I might not have been able to produce enough milk for Brendan, but I could still feed my family.

In so many ways, I was growing. I knew that having to work more with my hands and caring for a home was good for me. I would never be a perfect Swiss housekeeper with everything neat and tidy, but I was getting better. Michael definitely appreciated my cooking. It was more creative and fun than cleaning, so I was more motivated to work on it. Nevertheless, I did at times feel dragged down by the repetitive nature of the work, and still daydreamed about getting to do more of the things I really wanted to do.

Brendan was a joy, so funny and creative and active. Michael and I enjoyed taking him on trips to the mountains and the sea, and to visit our families in Seattle and Switzerland. We shared in his wonder and delight, his energy that impelled him to explore everything. We created our own round of festival traditions and celebrations for him, knitting us together as a family. We watched him play and imagine and grow, and it helped us to feel alive. My reluctance to have another child was about the image I had of myself as a bad mother, one who would be judged harshly for my failure with another newborn, rather than any reservations I had about my son. Only my underlying insecurity left me feeling not quite attached, still with one foot out of the door in case I needed to run away.

As at the threshold of Nain, two streams were confronting each other in me. Something old had to die, in order that something new could be born. I'd made a very small step toward speaking a truth I found shameful, and had viscerally felt how it brought release from a botched beginning. The cleansing stream of truth had to work upon me more and more, until it released me from the shame and fear that kept me in a frozen, deathlike state.

But for that, I needed much more intensive instruction. Fortunately, I was about to get it.

Meditation
Young man, I say to you, arise.

8.
A Demon-possessed Man in the Tombs:
Mark 5:1–20

No Name

I was the boy who had no name,
the one nobody wanted.
My mother was the scandal of the town,
passed around from man to man,
dragging me along,
unclaimed, unnamed.

When I was just able to toddle and cry
she went off with one of those nameless men.
Now I was the scandal of the town,
passed around from house to house,
briefly cared for,
then always abandoned.

When the voices began,
I welcomed them –

so I did have a family, after a fashion.
They told me strange things,
said to tear off my clothes,
draw blood from my skin.
But I didn't mind.
They filled me with strength
to resist the ones
who'd bind me in chains.
They filled my mouth
and cried out for me,
the words my childhood
had been denied.

They brought me to the edge,
away from those homes
where I'd never belonged,
those hearts of stone
where love had died.

The tombs were more friendly.
I lived there among the honest dead,
who didn't pretend
to be alive.

But my body remembered
another life,
a time – so brief! –
when I was caressed,
when I was held,
when I was wanted.

My body knew him when he arrived,
the one who'd crossed the sea of souls.
It toddled over to him and fell,
like an infant asking to be carried.

I had no words. But the crowd in me,
they cried out, they begged him, 'Do not hurt us!'

He asked for our name
and they gave it, my army,
my league of protectors,
my guard against the dark.

They gave themselves away, they gave me
back my life, so long ago stolen.
They went into the beastly bodies
borne over the edge, to be at rest.

The townsmen were cold and afraid as ever.
They couldn't bear life to arise from the tombs,
could not conceive of a nameless man
being reborn as a child of God.
But I am that man. I am his man now,
wherever he sends me to cry out his name
in the wilderness of empty hearts.
The name that can never be stolen again,
the name that is mine now, and yours.

I am.

Reflections on *A Demon-possessed Man in the Tombs*

At this point in the Synoptic Gospels, a shift takes place. So far, Jesus has been working in Galilee, moving around but centered in his 'own city' of Capernaum. Now, he starts to travel further. He does not yet go to Judea, but pushes the boundaries of his healing mission, moving into new realms of soul experience and relationship to his environment. As he goes, his disciples develop on their journey as well.

Seven healings have been described in Luke, five in Mark, and three in Matthew. They have addressed different aspects of the human organism; the true mission of the Hebrew people has been invoked; and, with the raising of the young man of Nain, ancient forms of initiation have been brought into play and the need for their renewal indicated.

At this point, Jesus and his disciples get into a boat and cross the Sea of Galilee. It is no ordinary, mundane trip that the three evangelists each describe. Jesus challenges the disciples to enter the spiritual realm that borders the physical world: the realm of life, where forces surge and interweave, threatening to overwhelm the unwary. This is necessary for the disciples' training as healers, but they do not pass the first test. They have to call upon Jesus to save them, waking him from sleep so that he can calm the storm. As he did in the first two healings, Jesus 'rebukes' (*epitimao*) the wind and the waves, bringing the elements back into harmonious balance. The disciples can only marvel at this power; they do not yet aspire to attain it themselves.

On the eastern side of the sea, in an area where steep cliffs border the water and ancient tombs are found among the hills, they encounter another demon-possessed man (or two men, in Matthew). Many non-Jews live here, as indicated by the presence of a herd of pigs. Jesus and his disciples have left the familiar, supportive surroundings of their religious community, and the phenomena that meet them are frightening. After the unsettling experience of the storm, here is a man who rages like a storm himself, who can break iron chains, and who does not wear human clothing or live in a house. Instead, he lives in the tombs, in a sub-human realm.

Again, as with the man with an unclean spirit, I have imagined a trauma that could have warped this man's humanity and caused him to behave so strangely. Early bonding with a consistent caregiver is now known to be the essential ground for mental, psychological and even physical health. A disruption to this bond leads to illness on every level, and the earlier the break, the harder it is to repair.[1] The adversarial forces that want to overpower humanity and bend us to their own use can easily enter in when such a weakness is present. This is precisely the sort of trauma that the social structure of the Israelite people was designed to prevent, with its injunctions to care for the widow and the orphan.

But Jesus looks past the sub-human appearance of this sufferer, and asks, 'What is your name?' The name of the demons may be Legion, but each person's name is 'I', echoing the name of the God of Israel: I AM THAT I AM. This drop of the Godhead within each individual must become active in order for healing to take place. Christ's question calls for the trauma-damaged person to recall his true I, which is still there beneath the layers of dysfunction. Behaviors stigmatized as 'demonic', or, in our current terms, psychotic, may only be defense mechanisms that have outlived their usefulness. The solution is to provide the much-needed safety and care for the lost and frightened child hiding within the apparent monster.[2] No matter how our earthly families and communities may fail us, our heavenly parent is still caring for us, and Christ has come into our earthly sheaths to restore the bond.

The strange image of the demons entering into a herd of pigs and plunging into the sea might be connected to the fact that the goddess Artemis was worshipped in this area, where ruins of a temple still remain above the ancient city of Gerasa. Boars were often sacrificed to Artemis, to honor her skill as a huntress. Non-human forces, whether they come from the more animalistic aspects of our soul or the elemental forces of nature, cannot be destroyed, but they must be kept in their proper place. Human beings are increasingly separating out their ego from those forces, which need and, on some level, want to be mastered by the human ego. I have imagined that the so-called 'demons' might have been in some way relieved to meet their match in Jesus, that their self-destruction was a kind of sacrificial gesture that released them, as well as the man they had been inhabiting.

The people of the area who witness this healing are not relieved, but terrified. Something of immense, incomprehensible power has come into their midst, and they do not like it. Christ Jesus has to leave this place on the periphery and return to the center of his activity in Galilee, but he encourages the man to tell of his experience throughout the area, making him in a sense one of the earliest apostles, those who are 'sent out' to spread the good news.

Personal Connections – Part 8

We arrived at Carrefour House[3] in the spring, just after Easter. The snow in New England was melting but still heaped up in shadowy hollows and corners. The bare earth was starting to turn green and to bloom with daffodils and crocuses, and the trees were fuzzed with new leaves. They would soon open and cover the hillsides with watercolor tones of rose pink, light green, yellow, orange: a pale, pastel reflection of the autumn glory to come.

The big, red barn-like house was set upon the shoulder of a mountain, perched on a slope that ran down to a brook trickling below. It belonged to an anthroposophical community for adults with developmental disabilities, inspired by Rudolf Steiner's indications for working with such individuals. Michael's job as a therapeutic eurythmist at the Waldorf School had been cut and he'd been freelancing, but we both needed more full-time employment. Brendan would be going into first grade in the fall, so it was a good time for him to make the switch. We thought the rural environment and community setting would be perfect for him.

I was trusting Michael to take the lead here. He was the one who had experience in caring for people with additional support needs. He'd trained in Switzerland and worked therapeutically with children in a school there, as well as with children and adults in the US. I had only spent a few months at the Camphill Eurythmy School in England, where I went for an internship after I graduated. There, for the first time, I met adults with developmental disabilities in a large community in Yorkshire, another gorgeous landscape of moors and farmland. I was charmed by the residents' openness and friendliness, and sometimes baffled by their strangeness. But I didn't engage deeply with them at that time, insulating myself in the eurythmy group and spending most of my free time exploring outside the community. I felt distinctly unskilled in an area where I considered Michael to be an expert.

Now I had signed on for a whole new journey. We had been hired to be the house-parents at Carrefour, caring for several resident adults, and supervising volunteers from overseas as our staff helpers. We would work together with the house-parents of the other houses to plan activities and run the community, bearing responsibility for all aspects of life in a large household: from cooking, shopping and laundry, to house repairs, maintenance, medical needs and recreation. It was my first full-time job since the Montessori school, and it was something for which I had no training or experience, other than my dubious skills as a housekeeper.

Yet I felt this was the right step for all of us. Brendan's tuition at the Waldorf school would be paid by the community, which also provided us room and board and full medical insurance, along with a monthly stipend. The place was marvelous for children, with its acres of fields and woods to explore, and our work would be 'at home' so we would not have to leave Brendan alone or in daycare. He could come along with us and not feel so lonely as an only child. I also wanted more hands-on work, rather than doing so much on the computer or with my intellect alone. I was intrigued by the residents, and wanted to learn more about how they manifested the spirit, in spite of the challenges that meant they could not survive on their own.

When we had come to interview for the job, we talked one evening with a coworker. I asked her what she thought was needed to do this work.

She pondered for a moment, and then said, 'Are you interested in people?' It was all about working with people. If you weren't interested in that, you wouldn't like it.

She added, 'Can you get in the shower with someone?' I took this to mean both a literal willingness to bathe people who couldn't do it by themselves, and a willingness to metaphorically immerse oneself in something, to let certain boundaries and defenses get washed away. To risk things getting slippery, maybe even a bit unstable.

In the six years to come, I was to experience in abundance the challenges brought by working with people in an immersive environment. Learning to wash people's bodies was the easy part. At first I was scared to hurt or frighten them, but I quickly learned that they were completely used to this kind of assistance, and showed me what to do when I made a mistake. More importantly, I myself was about to enter into an immense shower, where much would be washed away, sometimes with almost unbearable force. Much would be revealed, under the encrusted habits and defense mechanisms, the dysfunctional patterns that had built up in me and between me and the members of my family.

I knew, dimly, that my patterns were hurtful, both to myself and to other people, which wasn't what I wanted. I knew, deep down, that the anger that I'd sensed after 9/11 still flamed within me and had yet to be defused. It came out sometimes with Brendan, when I yelled at him over some minor lapse or failure to meet my expectations, though he was innocent and undeserving of this fury. I would apologize afterward, but that did not undo the hurt.

So I'd come to this place where our supposed mission was to help and teach and lead people who could not help themselves. But really, it was me who was most in need of help, and I was about to meet my greatest teachers.

The lessons started on my very first day.

'What's your name?' Colleen sat next to me on the couch, eyes wide behind thick glasses, brows raised in an expression of perpetual surprise. When I didn't respond immediately, she repeated, 'What's your name?' Each repetition grew higher and louder, as she craned her head toward me and edged closer on the cushions, pressing into my personal space.

I'd already answered, but I told her once more. 'I'm Lory. I'm your new housemother.'

A pause, and then again, 'What's your name?'

Colleen was about forty years old, tall and pale, with a short crop of bright orange hair that showed her Irish heritage. She talked incessantly, asking question after question without listening for the answers, repeating some over and over. What was she really looking for? Something behind the words, that my literal, language-bound, intellectual mind was unable as yet to grasp?

It was my first day as a house-parent and she was the first of the residents in our house to arrive after the spring vacation. I was alone with her and trying to find a way to communicate.

I had an idea. I ran upstairs to our apartment and fetched our wedding album. I sat next to Colleen and showed her the pictures of me and Michael and our friends and family, the dresses, the cake, the celebration dinner. The book formed a shield between us, but also contained images we could share, to link us together.

She liked this, and her restless queries stilled for a short time. But soon enough they began again: 'What's your name?'

As I gradually got to know the other residents in our house and the members of our community, I was challenged by even more different ways of speaking and acting, all unfiltered by our so-called 'normal' patterns of social interaction. Some individuals were talkative, others silent; some were greedy and some had to be coaxed into eating; some were constantly, restlessly active, and some sat without moving or, it seemed, perceiving what was going on around them.

But such appearances could be deceptive. Everything that happened affected our residents, not only our actions and words, but our thoughts and feelings, too. For example, if Colleen's excited chattiness met with boredom or inattentiveness, it could send her into a state of withdrawal that ended with her holed up in her room, refusing to come out or talk to anyone. Other residents reacted to a mood of tension or anxiety in the house with loud cries of distress, or by tearing up papers or clothing. Some coped with obsessive, repetitive speech and gestures, or by invading people's rooms and personal space.

Such behavior had to be modulated by the coworkers to protect everyone's rights, their property and safety. It was our job to create healthy rhythms and maintain boundaries, something the residents were unable to do for themselves. I didn't know a great deal about how to do that, but I would have to learn quickly.

Those who have little experience of developmentally disabled people often feel awkward or strange or frightened around them. They don't always know what to say or how to say it. Once, I might have felt the same way, but as I lived among them and got to know them, I started to resonate with them in ways I'd never anticipated or expected. I sensed that their true individuality, their 'I', though unable to express itself in the ways I was used to, was still there. Only their outer sheaths had become disjointed or out of order in some way, blocking communication, distorting the meaning behind the appearances. But when we met them with compassionate, empathetic engagement, invoking senses and capacities not called on in ordinary life, we could begin to see in each of them the light that shone within the bushel that shrouded it.

Caring for the residents started to wake up parts of me that also needed to be cared for, parts that I had exiled from my conscious mind and sent to live in isolation in the borderlands of my subconscious. Would I be able to accept them, and allow them to be seen and heard? And would I be able to accept those hidden exiles in other people who were not so open, unguarded, and honest as our residents, but were still fearfully trying to bury the monsters within?

This was the question that wordlessly posed itself now, a question that would determine the course of my future destiny. On the threshold of midlife, with decades of failure and error behind me, the possibility for renewal was beckoning. A new life was possible, if only I could find the courage to make the necessary sacrifice.

> *Meditation*
>
> What is your name?

9.
A Bleeding Woman and a Dying Girl:
Mark 5:21–43

Talitha, Koum

The Woman

I saw him from a distance,
moving through crowds, on his way
to save that poor little girl –
no, twelve years old, a child no more.
Time to enter a woman's life,
to pass through that gate of pain.

It was twelve years ago my own life ended.
I was caught out alone on a darkened night,
my cloak torn aside,
my maidenhood taken.

I couldn't speak of what had happened.
I knew how he would be believed,
and I, the temptress, condemned.
Then, two moons without blood –
I walked in fear
my secret would be discovered,
my shame revealed to all.

When the bleeding began,
at first I was glad – the life in me
had ended itself, no one would know,
and I'd not be caught again.
There was pain, but it passed;
bloody cloths, but I burned them,
and thought that was the end.

The next day, more blood. And the next –
and so on, and on, as everyone knows;
my hiding days were over.
They don't know why, but they do sense something
uncanny there, or cursed.

I could never be clean,
and no one could touch me
without soiling themselves –
no, not even the hem of my garment.
So my dark life flowed out,
abundant but useless,
love consumed by death.

Then I saw where he walked,
a bright star mobbed by clouds,
and a ray of hope pierced my darkness.
He, too, poured out life
from an endless source,
but no death reigned in him.

If I could just touch his shining,
come in range of that radiance,
my light might be rekindled,
my empty heart cease its weeping.

I'll not halt his healing of the maiden,
not show myself or speak,
just come close in the crowd
and reach out my hand,
nearer, nearer,
now…

The Maiden

The day they brought me my woman's gown,
bound up my hair, and made the rites
to mark my childhood's end,
my mother kissed me, spoke words of pride –
only I saw her tears.

My blood had come, that secret stain
that no man sees, and yet we women
announce it to all with these outward signs:
here's a new one ripe to wed and bear.

That's when I started to die a little,
as if some essence left my limbs
along with the bloody flow.
I couldn't speak of it, too ashamed
to say I might not have the strength
for shouldering a woman's lot
of suffering and care.
But day by day my life bled out,
and I walked in a dream, unaware how I went,
until I staggered and fell.

Laid out on the bed, as though in the tomb,
my spirit left my body.
I saw people like stars, most faint and dim,
a few souls blazing brighter.
Out in the market a great mob flickered,
and at its center –
a Sun.

All at once his flame
became too bright
for even my inner eye.

I saw no more,
swallowed up by the dark.
There was nothing then, no light, no sound.
Without feeling or fear, I rested.
Till in time beyond time the Sun spoke to me,
calling me maiden, bidding me rise.

How could I return
to that life I'd failed?
Wouldn't it happen again?
The bleeding, the losing,
the fainting, the dying?
Better to just float away.

Then his hand in mine,
and I felt flowing through it
a woman's courage, that no man can know:
courage to bear impossible life,
to strive against hope, and face down death
for the sake of a future unborn.

Love asked me to live,
and at last I could answer
Yes.

Reflections on *A Bleeding Woman and a Dying Girl*

After healing the demon-possessed man, Jesus returns with his disciples across the sea. In Matthew, several other incidents are inserted here, but in Mark and Luke the next healing follows at once: a double healing of a woman with an issue of blood and of the young daughter of Jairus, a leader of the synagogue in Capernaum.

The woman has been bleeding for twelve years, and the girl is twelve years old. To speak of a woman bleeding very likely refers to blood flowing from the womb, a menstrual disorder. A girl of twelve is on the threshold of puberty, but this maiden is having difficulty in crossing over into womanhood: she lacks the strength to transition into that new phase. These two female figures represent, respectively, an excess and a deficiency in the powerful life force that flows through the organs of reproduction and guides women through the changes of their cycle. Another imbalance has become ingrained, which can only find its healing through the mediating presence of Christ Jesus.

The woman, with her excess of life force, takes the initiative and oversteps the boundaries of what would have been permissible at the time. A woman was unclean during her menstrual period, and a constantly bleeding woman would be considered permanently unclean (see Leviticus 15:19–32). She could not touch or be touched by anyone without contaminating them; anything she sat or lay down on was also considered unclean. If a woman had a discharge outside of her period, once it was over she had to bring offerings to the priest as an atonement: 'Thus you shall keep the people of Israel separate from their uncleanness, lest they die in their uncleanness by defiling the tabernacle that is in their midst' (Leviticus 15:31). For the woman to reach out to touch anyone was a serious transgression of purity laws that were considered a guard against untimely death.

Jesus does not object to her daring act, however; he wants only to know who has touched him. Why does the woman come forward, knowing she has broken a religious law? Mark says that she knew 'what had happened to her' (Mark 5:33); Luke says that she 'saw that she was not hidden' (Luke 8:47). The 'straight way' proclaimed by Isaiah and John the Baptist is being constructed in and through her. The mysterious, dark, hidden ways of the reproductive cycle, representative of the bodily processes that work in us without our conscious awareness, have to be transformed into the light of thinking.

Though she is in fear and trembling, the woman tells 'the whole truth' (*aletheia*). This word indicates a lifting of the forgetfulness that comes over us when we cross the threshold of death, symbolized by the river Lethe in Greek mythology. Human beings need to become aware of the whole course of their destiny if they are to become co-creators with the divine world. We need to be able to compensate for the imbalances that we have created in our earthly lives, rather than having such compensation imposed upon us from outside.

The woman's willingness to reveal the whole truth about herself may be an expression of the 'faith' (*pistis*) that Jesus says has actually healed her. To have faith is to trust in divine love and goodness. Healing can only take effect when we let go of the fear that holds us imprisoned and open up to the good that guides our destiny, no matter how painful and incomprehensible it may appear at the moment. If we can persist patiently in spite of years of failure and suffering, and dare to reach out when we sense a healing power approaching, a sudden resurgence of energy is possible. Miracles are not events that overturn the laws of nature, but simply what happens when long-disjointed channels come back into alignment so that life can flow through them again.

From the woman, we turn to the girl. Her own life energy has ebbed, and she appears to have crossed the threshold of death. Jesus, however, says that she is only sleeping. 'Do not fear, only have faith' (*pisteuo*), he tells the child's father, echoing what has just happened with the woman. Fear must be replaced by trusting faith in the loving purposes of God.

Bringing only his three closest disciples, Jesus silences the noisy mourners and joins the girl's parents in an inner room. He takes the girl by the hand and, as with the paralyzed man, tells her to raise herself.

The Aramaic phrase '*Talitha, koum*' is only included in Mark's Gospel and means 'Maiden, stand up'. It is translated in Greek as 'Little girl, I say to you, arise' – the same formula found in the story of the raising of the young man of Nain and thus also a reference to the mysteries. *Talitha* is related to the Hebrew *taleh*, meaning lamb. Perhaps this maiden can be seen as an image of the sacrificial lamb that can no longer restore the link between humanity and the divine world. Its energy has been drained away, worn out before it can come into its life-giving strength. But Christ, the heavenly Lamb who sacrifices himself so that humanity can live, renews the offering and makes it real and effective again. The human child can stand up once more and grow into her potential.

The girl starts walking immediately, straightaway (*eutheos*): the 'straight way' is active in her as well. This happens now not only *within* a single person but *between* individuals. Through the wise working of destiny, people who need to resolve something that arises from the past are brought together, and a new stream of healing potential comes to life.[1]

Personal Connections – Part 9

Three and a half years after we'd arrived at Carrefour, Michael and I went to the Town Hall to cast our vote in the presidential election. It was Michael's first time voting in the US, since he had only recently become a citizen. We went through the procedure, stopping at the ID table staffed with retirees, through the dusty wood-panelled hall that was like a stage set for *Our Town*, then in and out of the creaky old booths as we cast our votes.

There's a photo from this day of us smiling in front of the booth run by the local Democratic organization, squinting against the sun, looking windblown and happy. We'd done our duty in keeping the world safe for democracy, in small-town New England, where American democracy had been born.

The rest of the day was the usual round of shopping and cooking and meetings and family duties. I went to bed that night without looking at the news. I kept away from news in general, finding it depressing and not helpful for coping with life. I'd find out in the morning how the election had turned out, although I had no doubt who would be our new president.

When I got up the following day, I checked my social media. Friends on Facebook were in a state of panic and shock. I could not believe what I read. How could this happen?

The effect on me of Donald Trump's election cannot be explained in rational terms. I felt as if I were thrown out of my body and could barely function. Rather than wanting to be with people, I became suspicious and distrustful of everyone I met, wondering if they were Trump supporters. I stopped at a gas station once and a man spoke to me in a friendly way about a scratch on the van door, telling me he knew a place where I could get it fixed. I glared at him suspiciously and edged slowly away, assuming he was an enemy somehow targeting me in this strange manner. I later saw him again at a Democrats' meeting, but for me at that time everyone was a Republican until proven otherwise.

The strangest thing was that I knew the Republicans felt the same way about people like me – they thought we were fearsome enemies to be avoided and shunned. And yet we were all just human beings, all the same under the skin. Why were we so afraid of each other?

At night, unable to sleep, I would go out into the field across from our house, look up at the cold New England stars and wonder what was happening to the world. I would do the gestures for the word 'hallelujah' in eurythmy – a healing exercise – and wordlessly cry out my anguish to the angels. How would our country survive this insanity?

There was nothing I could do about Trump's election. But there were patterns closer to home that I might be able to affect.

My muddled awareness that something was wrong, in me and in my life, was growing. Some messages got through, but they were fragmentary and mysterious. One night when I was out in the field, I thought, 'If I could do what I really wanted, be who I really am, I would be a priest.' Then the next thought came: 'But I can't, because of the split in my consciousness.'

Disturbing as this thought was, I sensed it was true. Although I might not have been diagnosed with a mental illness, nor did I ever fully lose my capacity to reason and think logically, I had long been bearing a deeply unhealthy split inside my soul. With my rational side, I focused on a small area of awareness that contained those thoughts and feelings I found permissible, and exiled everything else. Meanwhile, the dark, unpenetrated areas that rumbled underground, disturbing my physical and psychological health, only grew stronger and more troublesome.

The split between these two realms was keeping me from becoming who I really was. It excluded me from the realm of holiness and the work of spreading the Gospel. How had it come into being? Could it be healed?

On the third night, the thought came to me, 'I cannot carry the burden of the whole world. I have to take up my own task and trust in the spiritual world to carry the rest.'

Then I was able to resume more or less normal operations in daily life. But these night-time revelations felt like going through a baptism, a frightening trial by water or by fire, after which a new life had to begin. New, demanding questions opened up. What was my task, anyway? And who was I, split as I was, to perform it? What could I do that would not merely bring more chaos into the world?

The woman and the maiden healed by Christ, brought together through his balancing, reconciling presence, had to come together in me, too. The parts that were overflowing and the parts that were exhausted, the parts that were too much and the parts that were too little, had to turn toward each other and start working for a common goal, joining the stream of true humanity. I could not yet see how to do that, but the trumpet had sounded. It was time to awaken and rise.

> *Meditation*
> Do not fear, only have faith.

10.
A Gentile Woman's Daughter:
Matthew 15:21–28

Crumbs

They called us dogs, fit to be kicked
and spat on, as they'd never do
to their own hounds.

But we were mangy, mongrel curs,
tainted and corrupt,
following foreign gods.

They allowed us to live
on the edges of their land,
gleaning the remnants of their fields,

but never to mix
with their own sacred children,
the heirs of Abraham's promise.

My mother and I kept to ourselves,
meekly curling our tails,
trying to mind our own business.

But a pack of the pure ones followed me home
as I came one day from the market,
basket full of our daily bread –

a group of boys from the synagogue,
punching and daring each other,
taunting and whistling and laughing.

They came too close. I hurried faster,
and they sped up. I was hot with fear,
not knowing what they'd dare.

I was running now, and the pack pursued me.
No longer seeing where I went,
I turned a corner blind, and tumbled

into a hole, a builder's quarry
lined with sharp rocks and sliding gravel
that tore and pierced as I fell.

The boys stopped, breathless, on the edge.
My basket lay empty, all the bread
tumbled out and scattered.

They stared open-mouthed, then turned and ran.
The loaves were crushed under heedless feet
and I lay like them, broken to crumbs.

One boy remained. He scrambled down,
and asked where I lived, if he could bring someone
to help me, my people, my kin.

I croaked out some words. He ran off and returned
with some neighbors of mine,
who brought me to my mother.

She wept and wailed as she tended me,
cursing the wolves who'd do this crime,
who would let me die in a hole.

She wondered if they'd ever heard
the story of Ruth, our kinswoman
from whose line was birthed their King.

I didn't care what stories they knew.
Though her curse invoked demons to punish the boys,
the demons settled in me.

The hole opened up as I ran each night,
pursued by a pack of furious dogs,
and I fell, and fell, and fell.

On the third day my mother heard of a teacher,
one of theirs, who wandered about
like a homeless dog himself,

sometimes received, sometimes repulsed.
A master of demons is not always welcome –
you don't know what he brings with him.

So she sought his aid, her rage bundled up
like loaves in a basket, begging most humbly,
but when he refused, she broke.

'Even the dogs eat the children's crumbs!'
she snapped out, then went pale and afraid.
How would he punish her now?

But he only laughed, and said she was right,
and I was healed. The dogs trotted off,
obeying some call I couldn't hear,

and from a body in a grave
I turned to a seed at rest in the earth,
awaiting my own call to life.

We follow him now, my mother and I,
leaving our kin, just as Ruth did.
We are gleaners of truth, gathering crumbs.

His way leads to home, and rest, and peace,
even if it must pass through death.
I've been there, and I know.

Reflections on A Gentile Woman's Daughter

The story of the Gentile woman and her demon-possessed daughter takes place on the fringes of the land claimed by the Israelites, calling up old animosities and fears of boundary violation. It follows a long discourse in which the Pharisees and scribes complain that Jesus and his disciples are not following the traditions and commandments of their religious community. Jesus explains to them that it is not what touches the body or enters through the mouth that defiles a person, but what comes from the heart, from the inner human being. Physical substances and actions must be transformed into an inner perception of soul and spiritual processes.

Jesus demonstrates this through his own willingness to listen to and learn from a woman who is an outsider to the Jews. Through this healing, Jesus makes oblique reference to the task of the Israelite people. The Israelites were God's 'Chosen People' not because they were meant to reside permanently at the top of a hierarchical structure, still less to be bullies who kept others down, but rather to be leaders in a development in which all of humanity was to participate. They were to develop the relationship to the God whose name is I AM THAT I AM, to the ego-principle, which not everyone can manage at the same pace. But as mentioned in Chapter 6, the promise to Abraham was that everyone, all the nations of the earth and not just those who descended from the patriarch, would receive a blessing through this relationship. It was the Israelites' dedication to becoming a blessing for others that would keep them in alignment with the special mission to which they had been called.

Over the course of history, however, this aspect of the mission had become obscured by animosity toward other nations – in much the same way that establishing and defining our own ego often leads us to criticizing other human egos we see as opposing us. For a time, the Israelites did have to establish their dominance in the land. The spiritual individuality, working its way into the physical world, was creating its own first-half-of-life container. But by the time of Jesus, this container had lost much of its integrity. The nation had been divided by internal conflict, defeated and humiliated by the surrounding nations and, ultimately, made subject to the supreme power of Rome. For anyone who suffers in this way, it is a common response to seek internal security by increasing the sense of 'otherness' regarding people who are perceived as different.

Such feelings serve to strengthen and define an individuality, or an ethnic group. Customs and traditions, rigorously observed, also serve this function. During the time of the Babylonian captivity, for example, when the Jewish religion actually took shape, it wasn't possible to worship in the Temple. But it was possible to keep the Sabbath, maintain the dietary laws and practice circumcision. All of these things became more important, as a way of maintaining a people's identity when surrounded by foreigners.[1]

But with the appearance of Christ, all that changed. The outer fight had now to become an inner battle, signifying the change in the course of evolution that Christ came to help us navigate. As Jesus said in the Sermon on the Mount, now we must love our enemies and pray for them. That is the new way of Christ, and it is a hard one to follow.

The woman, who in Mark is called a Greek and described as being Syrophoenician by birth, reminds Jesus that the blessing of the 'children' is for all people and not only for those who lead the way – something he should know quite well. He responds, 'For this statement you may go your way.' The term translated as 'statement' is *logos*, the creative Word that has already shown its healing power in the story of the centurion's servant. Now, not only a foreigner, but a woman who would normally have no voice at all, dares to speak a word that redirects Jesus to his own true mission. It's an incredibly innovative and brave act.

In Matthew, the woman is called a Canaanite, recalling the story of Ruth, a Moabite woman who became the grandmother of King David. Ruth is one of four women named in Matthew's genealogy of Jesus, all of whom belonged to tribes that were enemies of the Israelites – a subtle dig at nationalism. In Matthew's version of the healing story, the woman calls Jesus 'Son of David', making an explicit connection with that lineage. Matthew also changes and expands the story – which is unusual, as most of his healings are condensed versions of those in Mark – to reflect the pattern given in the book of Ruth. The widowed Ruth begs her mother-in-law, Naomi, three times to let her go back with her to her homeland, vowing that she will take on Naomi's God, the God of Israel, as her own. The Canaanite woman has to plead three times for Jesus to hear her request, and cheekily asserts that even foreign 'dogs' have the same right to be fed as the children of Israel.[2]

In Matthew and Mark, this healing takes place following the Feeding of the Five Thousand, a landmark event in all four gospels. There, it has been shown how the disciples are learning to perceive the spiritual food that streams out from Christ, and to become channels for conveying it to others. 'You give them something to eat,' the disciples are told (Matthew 14:16; Mark 6:37; Luke 9:13). Everyone needs this living substance, but not everyone can access it directly. It is therefore essential that Christ have students who advance themselves solely so that they can serve others who are further behind.

As his ministry expands further, Jesus shows himself to be a healer of those rifts between human beings that become enshrined in tradition and culture, the unjust hierarchies that aim to keep some people permanently subject to others. He liberates us from the mental habits that keep us bound in prisons made of fear, and is not himself afraid to model this transformation by changing his own mind.

Personal Connections – Part 10

Michael was not as disturbed as I was by the election of Trump. He thought the whole crazy political circus was ridiculous, but he didn't feel the same existential threat that I did.

Just after the inauguration in January, I was in a state of hysteria. I'd been hoping that some kind of miracle would prevent the coming disaster, but it didn't. I started ranting to Michael about the evil I was experiencing; he said afterwards that he feared I was going crazy. I remember being at a sort of a crossroads and having to decide whether I went this way or that: away from Michael and into my own world of fearful alarm, or back down into my body, trying to stay in communication with him, no matter how impossible it seemed.

I chose to stay.

I stopped raving and tried to get a grip on myself, but I still didn't know how to talk about my feelings. Then, one night, Michael complained that I never talked to him; he didn't know what was going on with me. At the time I hadn't believed he wanted to know, but apparently he did. This gave me the permission to talk that I had not known I needed.

I started as we were driving to Boston on our way to see a show. I talked during the intermission and I talked more on the way back. I do not remember what I said, but I do remember that feeling of release and the relief. Afterwards, Michael said it was as though I 'broke open'.

And Michael welcomed it. He was ready to receive it. He began to talk as well, telling me things he'd never told me before. We started to have long, late-night conversations that were incredibly intimate, charged with creative energy, yet of an innocent tenderness that was like something from before the Fall. It was like going back to how our souls had mingled before birth, how we had known each other before the veils descended.

I was so touched, so impressed, by what I heard. There were so many things he'd probably told me before that I had not taken in, back in the early days of our relationship when I was preoccupied with his love as a salve for my pain. Now I understood at last that he had his own pain that was not yet resolved, causing him to hurt me without truly intending to, putting up barriers between us that now appeared to have dissolved. At last we could see each other in a new way that was really our original, true way of being.

He learned things he hadn't known about me, either. I told him about my depression after Brendan was born, my fears about being an unloving person, my dread at the miscarriage. I told him how hurt I had been by his anger and coldness, how that had made me retreat into myself and away from him.

He was sorry that he hadn't realized at the time how I felt, but it had been a hard time for him, too. I found out how much he had hated his job, how much pressure he'd always felt to soldier on and pretend to be stronger than he was. When we'd gotten together, it was in part because he sensed I was a spiritually strong person. When I broke down, it had shocked him and he'd been unable to handle it except by turning away and blaming me. Now, though, he said he understood.

Our love life became richer and deeper in every way. In fact, it was only at this point that I could actually say I fell in love with Michael for the first time. When we met, I had not been able to love anybody, traumatized and frozen as I was. At last, the wedding promises we had made seemed to be coming true. It was a rapturous experience.

Too bad it could not last.

As our sacred time of sharing ended and slowly faded into the past, I was left with a new sensitivity to what lived within and between us.

I began to believe that Michael was suffering from an undiagnosed form of depression, even though he resisted using that term to describe himself. When he talked about how he had to bide his time and find what pleasure he could until death released him from a life that had been irrevocably botched, I felt as though I were staring into a black hole of unhealed grief. Certain events from his childhood, which he didn't seem to consider especially concerning, seemed to me to represent serious trauma that had never been addressed. In order to survive, he'd dismissed and ignored his own pain. When this dark, depressed side was first revealed to me after Brendan's birth, I'd egotistically taken it as a personal criticism and withdrawn, keeping silent in order to protect myself. Thus I'd missed the chance to learn more about what was really behind his sudden, shocking change in attitude and behavior.

But now I saw things differently. I didn't believe that such pain was not cause for concern, that it had to simply be endured, or that there was no way out except death. Now that I'd let my guard down his pain was my pain, and if he didn't want to do anything about it, I did. In fact, my desire to help became an overwhelming compulsion. I was overpowered by surging emotions and unmanageable impulses, and as I started to urge Michael toward a healing he didn't agree he needed, new misunderstandings arose.

This was what my frozen state of soul had been trying to prevent. But I couldn't go back to that place. I had to go on and try to become strong enough to bear this life.

Over the following months, Michael and I were pulled together by our longing for loving connection and pushed apart by our fears and weaknesses. Words, which had briefly been windows into each other's souls, became barriers and weapons again. Michael sulked and retreated into dark moods; I sobbed and cried in desperation, but my displays of emotion only served to push him further away. We would briefly reconcile, seeking the nourishing flow of human relationship, then burst apart again, defending ourselves from the other's wrong interpretations and judgments.

Brendan was the true victim in all this, of course, and although we tried not to act out our difficulties in front of him, he surely felt them. We argued about how to care for him. Michael thought I should subjugate my own feelings and put 'the family' first, but that made me feel violated and used. I thought that Michael should let down his stubborn pride and seek counseling, but he resisted, not wanting to open up those dark forces he'd been hiding from everyone except me for so long. Our differences seemed irreconcilable, but we stayed together for the sake of a child we were pulling apart between us.

There were times when I felt as though one part of my mind was suppressing and disallowing another, keeping me from the truth. On one occasion, I was feeling utterly useless because Michael had once more rejected my overly emotional efforts to help him. For a moment, losing my role as his supporter in life seemed to mean I was worth nothing at all. But then I thought, 'No, that is not right.' I was an amazing person! I thought of all the things I had been through in my life and all the ways I had learned and grown. Even if Michael completely withdrew his approval from me, it didn't matter. I could still have esteem and appreciation for myself, no matter what anyone else thought.

This was a turning point that made me feel grateful for the shake-up of our marriage. I had become so dependent upon Michael for emotional sustenance that I had subjugated my own needs to his and almost lost my real self. Our crisis had forced me to stand on my own feet and become independent in terms of my own self-worth. That was a tremendous gift.

In some of his negative moods Michael would tell me what kind of person I was, or tell me what I could or could not do, even silly things like saying that I could never be a car mechanic when I expressed a passing interest. In the past I would have mutely accepted such statements, but now I started to resist. Who was he to define my possibilities and limit my choices? I was not going to tolerate it anymore. On the other hand, I could see that I also had fixed ideas about him that limited his possibilities. I had to give those up if I were to be true to my own principles.

Another time, when I brought up the idea of marriage counseling, he told me we could not do that, 'because it would be hell for Brendan'. I started nodding my head, thinking, 'No, of course not, we mustn't disturb Brendan.' But then I thought, 'Wait, what? The whole point is to make things better for Brendan, and for all of us. We can't just leave things the way they are!' I might not be able to convince Michael, but I had to become more awake within myself and resist the pull of such untrue thoughts.

I also caught myself thinking that I had no friends. Michael had been my closest companion for so many years, and in my busy and somewhat isolated life I'd lost contact with many others. Then I thought, 'No, wait, I *do* have friends!' At last I had begun to lose the shame that had kept me from opening up to people I knew truly cared about me. I began to call them and ask them for help, even if I could not convince Michael of his own need.

This shift in me occurred largely due to the example set by the residents in our community, who demonstrated that needing help did not necessarily result in exile or isolation. Rather, the whole community was built upon the principle of each person's needs being seen and met, while their unique gifts were appreciated and given a place to shine. I could not serve this ideal outwardly without it also working inwardly upon me, changing me and bringing healing.

One time when I was feeling especially lonely and hopeless, I was sitting in the community hall during our weekly folk-dancing session. The whole community would gather and dance to piano music, with residents aided by coworkers and volunteers. For many residents, this hour was a highlight of their week.

The dances were simple and unexciting, a round of familiar choices that after a few weeks bore no surprises. But the joy and pleasure of the residents, the way they delighted in the chance to move and be in rhythmic connection with others, was lovely to see. Nobody was forced to dance, but if someone was sitting out or looking unsure, someone else would try to invite or accompany them. Those who could move helped those who were more restricted in their movements. If someone was in a wheelchair, they could be pushed. Even just standing and rocking back and forth, or simply smiling, was a way to participate. There was no judgment; no one was found wanting or not good enough. There was only the embrace of the dance, holding and uniting all of us.

I sat there with tears in my eyes, thinking how beautiful it was. For so long, I'd been afraid of putting a step wrong and being thrown out of the dance. I'd been shaken by the many times I'd been criticized and found wanting by other people and, more importantly, the way I'd judged and rejected myself. But in this dance, the Sacred Dance of healing and reconciliation, there were no wrong steps. There was no mistake one could make that could not be taken up in love and incorporated into the whole.

This was the Kingdom of Heaven, right here on earth. This was what I had been looking for all my life, and if Michael and I had lost it in our marriage, that didn't mean it was gone for good. I could know that somewhere, somehow, the dance would always be going on, and that I was invited. Always.

Like the Canaanite woman who dared to speak up for her daughter's rights, I was beginning to feel that I had a right to exist and to be heard, whatever I had done wrong in the past. I might have made terrible mistakes, but that did not mean that I *was* a mistake. The residents of our community had taught me that with the testimony of their own lives. They lived in defiance of a worldly view that saw them as burdens on society who should be kept on the fringes, barely tolerated and dismissed.

Instead, I knew that each of them was a beloved child of God, heir of the Kingdom, in equal measure with each and every other human being. And I, too, was part of this company. I just had to conquer the voices that sought to lead me astray with their false accusations, and take up the blessing that was my birthright.

> *Meditation*
>
> For this word you may go your way.

11.
A Deaf Man:
Mark 7:31–37

Be Opened

When the voices of those around me
grew distant and faint, then ceased altogether,
as I saw their mouths flap open and shut,
blank doorways leading nowhere,
it only sealed the lonely tomb
I'd already lived in so long.

I'd always been shy, always stiff and unsure
in my own speech, hesitant, scared to risk
exposure of my soft, fragile core
to those who would mock and condemn it.

There were so many rules to follow,
so many ways I could fail and be punished,
and I never seemed to know what they were
till I'd crossed some line, and been jeered at.

So I hid. I kept silent.
I closed myself off.
Opening up was a way to be hurt.
I shut those doors
to keep myself safe –
in numbness was my defense.

And when my ears grew numb as well,
it gave me more space to be alone.
I retreated into the inner room
where death alone could release me.

But they wouldn't allow me,
those very ones
who'd laughed and taunted me the most –
they dragged me off,
frowning and pointing,
shouting words I could not hear.

I feared some new and terrible torture.
But they only brought me before a man,
a quiet man, standing so silent,
his love spoke louder than words.

It spoke to me as he took me aside,
away from that grimacing, gesturing crowd,
and as he touched me, ears and tongue,
anointing me with his own tongue's silence.

It said:
You are safe now.
I understand.
I know you, without your having to speak
a single word, without the risk
of your tenderness being torn and trampled.
Receive me now as your sheath, your self.
Have no fear.
Take courage.
Be opened.

And so I loosened my ears and my tongue.
I heard, I spoke, and saw my friends,
the ones I'd thought my enemies,
astonished, unable to still their own tongues,
for the wonder of it,
the unspeakable joy.

But as I now am able to speak,
I also know how to be silent.
I remember his way, his quiet way
of listening me back to life.

In silence I hear his voice again,
and open to his word.

Reflections on *A Deaf Man*

The Feeding of the Five Thousand is followed by more healings in Matthew and Mark, and then by another feeding, this time of four thousand (this whole section is absent from Luke). Matthew refers to a group healing of many blind, disabled and mute individuals, while in Mark, there is the wonderful and unique story of a deaf man with a speech impediment whose friends bring him to be healed as Jesus is passing through the region of the Decapolis on his way back to Galilee.

The method of healing in this encounter is more intimate and viscerally tactile than any Jesus has so far employed. Not only does he lay hands on the man, he puts his fingers in his ears and touches the man's tongue with his own saliva. He looks up to heaven, sighs, and says '*Ephphatha*', which is Aramaic for 'be opened'.

This touching of the man's tongue with saliva is startling, because people today have learned to be afraid of all bodily fluids as a source of contamination. Saliva is indeed a major carrier of disease, as it can transport microorganisms from one person to another. But the newest research shows that killing off or isolating ourselves from all such microorganisms is not the answer.[1] Our life in the body depends upon a finely differentiated, harmoniously interweaving community of microorganisms, of which only a small fraction are harmful, and are normally kept in check by a host of beneficial flora. Unfortunately, very few people in the Western world today are in this 'normal' state, as antibiotics and disinfectants and simply not having much contact with dirt have radically altered and depleted our microbiota.

The spittle of Christ Jesus, one can only imagine, is a substance of perfect balance capable of restoring harmony rather than causing disease. In a gesture of solidarity and communion with suffering humanity that will reach its apex on the cross, he gives of his own 'life-community' to the ill person.

The word translated as 'sigh' or 'groan' is *stenazo*, a peculiar word used only twice in Mark and nowhere else in the gospels. The other occurrence is after the Feeding of the Four Thousand, when the Pharisees demand a sign from Jesus to test him, and he 'sighs deeply' in response. It is found in the Epistles, for example in Romans 8:23: 'And not only the creation, but we ourselves, who have the first fruits of the Spirit, groan inwardly as we wait eagerly for adoption as sons, the redemption of our bodies.' The work of Christ Jesus to reunite humans with their spiritual origin is becoming intense, as his way and the way of the human being challenged to wake up to initiation-consciousness are coming together. More and more, the divine Christ being is uniting with the corporeal sheath of Jesus, the depth of his effort expressed with this vocalization.

There is a somewhat different aspect to the healings of a man with a speech impediment in Matthew and Luke, and the healing of another blind man who has difficulty speaking in Matthew. Each time, a demon is held responsible for the muteness, and the Pharisees or other onlookers accuse Jesus of casting out demons by means of demonic forces. This phrase, 'By the prince of demons he casts out demons,' is also found in Mark, though it is not connected to the healing of the deaf man, but rather to an earlier incident after Jesus calls the twelve and is rejected by his own family (Mark 3:22).

These stories indicate that our ability to speak is threatened by forces that are striving to knock us out of our most truly human selves and disrupt the healing mission. In the Psalms, we often read of people who are robbed of their speech and hearing when under stress, when they feel endangered and beset by enemies: 'I was mute and silent; I held my peace to no avail, and my distress grew worse'

(Psalm 39:2); 'I am like a deaf man; I do not hear [my enemies], like a mute man who does not open his mouth' (Psalm 38:13). Trauma, again, often stops people from speaking; it actually shuts down the language portion of the brain.[2] The resulting communication difficulties can lead to misunderstandings with others, and further isolation and suffering.

But sometimes, after a period of silence, speech returns and is all the more powerful for it. The poet Maya Angelou wrote in her memoir *I Know Why the Caged Bird Sings* of how she stopped speaking for years after she was sexually assaulted as a child.[3] Painful as this was, it became the wellspring of her poetic gift; in time she could turn pain into words of searing beauty. So also the people at the end of the healing of the deaf man rejoice, saying of Jesus, 'He has done all things beautifully and well' (*kalos* means both beautiful and good, both an aesthetic and moral quality).

It is not a lightly won achievement. Christ Jesus enters into the painful isolation and separation of humanity, and helps us to turn suffering into art – the art of living.

Personal Connections – Part 11

Michael and I had reached a point at which language felt more like a barrier between us than a bridge. He kept saying that we didn't understand each other and needed to talk, but whenever I tried, the words only caused more problems, more wounds. It was as though we were speaking different languages, even though they both sounded like English.

This was deeply frustrating because I relied on language to make sense of the world. Beneath my own habits of silence and withdrawal was a great longing to speak, and when Michael gave me permission to talk to him I thought that longing had finally found an outlet. Now I was learning that it wasn't so simple. Even after I'd overcome the nervousness that had prevented me from speaking before, some pre-verbal dysfunction was still there that distorted my power to verbalize thought. It meant Michael and I were unable to meet on the level of objective reality.

In spite of Michael's continued complaints that caring for my own development was a form of selfishness that distracted me from my duty to the family, I went away for a weekend to a workshop at the Alcyon Center on Mount Desert Island in Maine. In that beautiful, peaceful place, run by two women committed to the contemplative life, I learned practices of silent prayer and body-based mindfulness meditation that touched a deep, unmet need within me.

Although I'd been involved with the spiritual path of anthroposophy for many years, I'd never felt able to practice it as a method of inner work. I always faltered and gave up, perhaps afraid of what I might encounter within. Years ago, my doctor had told me there was something I didn't want to face, and I still hadn't figured out what it was. Even with the support of the sacraments of the Christian Community, I did not feel able to pray on my own, and I was frequently distracted and unfocused during the communion service. I took all of this as more evidence of how weak and useless I was, how I lacked the strength to overcome my inner obstacles.

Now, spurred on by the incredible pain that threatened to destroy my life, I found a new opening. Among a group of people who had dared to make themselves vulnerable and admit their brokenness (several of them were recovering drug addicts), I learned that my inner restlessness could be stilled when I focused on my body, letting it simply be, rather than trying to wrest it into line with my idea of how it should be. Eurythmy school had encouraged me to do the latter, but only as an extension of the mind–body split that dominates our Western culture.

We learn early on that there something is wrong with our bodies. We are expected to control and master them, and to keep them from overpowering the thinking with which we manage our world. Our bodies are only able to respond to this misguided view through symptoms, illness and dysfunction.

The true wisdom of the body is silent, yet it speaks to us all the time. We've got to start listening again to what speaks in the silence. At Alcyon, I gained practical tools for accessing that wisdom, and it soon became a lifeline for me.

This was another truth that the residents in our community were teaching me. They did not use language in the ways that I had been used to. It was not possible to communicate with them in the superficial, intellectual discourse that is our default mode today. I had to listen hard to understand what was behind their words, when they even used words at all. When a person says 'I' to mean 'you' and vice versa, when the words aren't clear or they mean something other than what you expect, it requires a giant leap in our intuitive capacities in order to communicate.

One of my trials-by-fire came during the first day of my new job as a house-parent, when I was undertaking the seemingly simple task of putting one of our residents to bed. Mark, an intensely determined man with few spoken words but many ritualistic observances, had been safely stowed beneath the covers and now I just had to turn off the lights. I pressed the button on the lamp and he popped up out of bed.

'No, no!' he cried and turned the light back on.

Did he not want me to turn it off? Did he sleep with the lights on?

But then he commanded me urgently, 'Turn it off, turn it off.'

After a few minutes of these off-and-on antics, I had the bright idea of flipping the switch on the wall, which, as it turned out, was connected to the lamp – and yes! This was what he had wanted me to do. Peace descended at last.

It was clear that I had a lot to learn, and that it had nothing to do with intellectual thinking, which sees no difference between turning off the light with a bedside button or with a switch on the wall. Intellectual achievement had always been my highest goal, but there is a truth beyond intellectual knowledge, a language beyond words, and it is this that we must begin to learn, lest our world fall to destruction. In this schooling, the residents were the masters, and I their humble student.

It is by caring for others, by wanting to perceive who they are and what they need independent of our own prejudices and fixed ideas, that we enter on this path of learning. By trusting me with their vulnerability, showing with their bodies and behavior what they could not express in words, the residents were challenging me to develop new capacities, new eyes and ears that could bring together again what had become separated in sensory existence.

It wasn't that life with our residents was always easy, or that their messages arrived in a lofty, pure, angelic way. I was frequently irritated and even frightened by their behaviors: the times they would pee on the floor, empty the soap dispensers, scream in the middle of the night, rip up their pillows, or stick their hands in excrement or cleaning fluid. Trying to meet their medical needs was especially challenging when they could not talk about them; it meant trying to read their inner state from cues like body language, skin tone and breathing patterns. I often had no idea what the meaning of their behavior was, or what to do about it, and yet I had to make some attempt if our household were to know any peace at all.

The residents never intended to annoy or scare me. They communicated in the only way they could, and it was up to me to understand them. If I succeeded about ten percent of the time, it was a step up from nothing. And the effort was also bringing about a needed change in me, an ability to listen to parts of myself that had long gone unheard.

Even though they reacted with immediate and transparent honesty to my mistakes, I knew that the residents always forgave me, and would always give me a chance to try again. Living in that atmosphere of forgiveness and acceptance of things-as-they-are was moving me toward the prayerful mood that is rooted in asking forgiveness for our weaknesses and faults, rather than hardening ourselves against criticism. The residents didn't wear that armor. They didn't apologize or try to justify themselves. They simply were who they were, and with that as my example it seemed possible that I could become who I really was, too. It was like being bathed in a lubricating fluid, which allowed things that had been stuck and frozen in the wrong place to start to move again.

One day, I was preparing lunch with a resident who would come over every week from another house to cook with me. Maria was a dynamic Latina woman who intimidated me at first by her tendency to pull everyone she met into a wild salsa dance party. I soon figured out that if I shook my head playfully at her from a safe distance, she would stop, and after that we developed a lovely relationship. But I was still unsure how to interpret some of her words and gestures.

As I was setting out the lunch plates and getting ready to serve the food, she appeared in the doorway of the dining room, pulling at her hair, scratching her arms, and moaning something. What was wrong? Had I not been paying enough attention to her? Did she need a hug, or reassurance that yes, we were having dessert? I got her to sit down on the couch and stop hurting herself, but she still looked deeply uncomfortable.

As I stared at her in perplexity, I suddenly heard the music that was playing. The CD changer had switched discs without my noticing it, going from a classical mix to some strange, piercing composition with twanging strings and bagpipes. Was this the source of Maria's discomfort?

I put on the Beatles instead, and she relaxed back into the cushions and smiled at me. Lunch proceeded without further disturbance.

I felt as though I had passed some kind of test. There was nothing in Maria's vocalizations or behavior to indicate that the music was what was bothering her, yet by momentarily slipping into her place, trying to feel what she was feeling, I had intuited something that defied intellectual understanding.

Like the deaf man who is met in such an intimate way by Christ, I was learning from the example of those who open themselves trustingly to the will of the Father, enabling the creative Word to speak in them again. My hardened defenses were starting to come down, and new possibilities were opening up. Truth was there to be heard, in the healing silence, in the world beyond words.

> *Meditation*
> Be opened.

12.

A Blind Man:

Mark 8:22–26

Double Vision

Before I lost my eyesight
I saw double –
as if there were two windows
into different worlds,
one rich and active, always moving,
nothing separate or fixed.
Rocks and stars, people and trees,
beasts and flowers
becoming each other, flowing in
and out and through.
A living world.

The other, a place of division and death.
All things separate.
People alone.
Dry and clean,

a desert space.
Like the one our people journeyed through,
a world without trees,
on our way to claiming
our promised land.

I didn't know how to put these together.
I shut one eye and then the other,
but that didn't help. What I saw with was not
my outer eyes, but some trick of the mind,
and mine was driving me mad.

What was real, what was true?
Life, or death?
Movement, or stillness?
Unity, or division?
How could these two
become one again?

When the world went dark
I knew I'd been given
a chance to find out.
Remove the veiling screen of sense,
and you see what is real
where it lives, in thought.
I sat and pondered
and saw in spirit.

I saw how our world
of trees and stones

that seem so hard and separate
is one with the world
from which it arose,
the world where there is no division, no death –
only endless change,
one form to another,
eternal evolution.
And I saw how our minds
in the desert of sense
are refined and honed
to be instruments,
clean and free,
through which this world
can know itself.

I saw, I knew.
But I was alone.
I could not share
my great new vision
with my sighted friends
who could not see.
We could never live
in the same bright world,
the world that had come to me
in darkness.

As I sat, sad and mute,
my friends came to me
and brought me to stand before a man,

a man who, I sensed, could see as I saw,
who knew what I knew, and knew me.

He led me away,
alone with him.
He spoke with his hands
before his words,
anointing my eyes
with his purity,
touching me
with his gentleness.
'Do you see anything?'
I opened my eyes.
Oh no – the double vision was back,
with walking trees and sprouting men.
But after his hands on me once more
the two flowed into one,
and at last I saw clearly
in this world's light.

He told me I might not be able to share
my vision with the village.
He said they were not ready yet
to understand, to see with new eyes.
But in time, he promised,
they too could be healed.

I don't mind waiting,
now that I know
I am not alone.

I know the new man
is walking through the desert,
walking
toward
his tree.

Reflections on *A Blind Man*[1]

In Mark, the second feeding of the multitude, the Feeding of the Four Thousand, is framed by two sensory healings: it is preceded by the healing of the deaf man and followed by the healing of the blind man of Bethsaida, a town on the northern shore of the Sea of Galilee. According to Luke, the Feeding of the Five Thousand took place near Bethsaida, which provides a slight link with this healing that he does not otherwise describe.

In Matthew and Mark, with the Feeding of the Four Thousand, Jesus gives the disciples further practice in serving a eucharistic meal. Even after their previous experience, they still question him about how so many people are going to be fed. But they take the food that he blesses and breaks, and serve it out, again making available to the crowd the outflowing forces of Christ.

That this is not a purely physical act is made clear by what follows soon after. As they cross the Sea of Galilee the disciples worry that they only have one loaf of bread with them. When Jesus says, 'Beware of the leaven of the Pharisees', they think he is talking about their single loaf, but he is warning them against the teachings of the Pharisees. In Matthew, Christ makes this clear by referring to the Feeding of the Five Thousand and the Four Thousand, symbolic images of his own spiritual teachings. What should be food for their souls, the disciples still confuse with material substance. In Mark, Christ says to them:

> 'Why are you discussing the fact that you have no bread? Do you not yet perceive or understand? Are your hearts hardened? Having eyes do you not see, and having ears do you not hear?' (Mark 8:17–18)

In a strange and difficult process, one must become blind and deaf to one world in order to awaken to another, and sometimes this can seem like being doomed to blindness altogether. The prophet Isaiah was told by the Lord to say to the people:

> 'Keep on hearing, but do not understand; keep on seeing, but do not perceive.' Make the heart of this people dull, and their ears heavy, and blind their eyes; lest they see with their eyes, and hear with their ears, and understand with their hearts, and turn and be healed. (Isaiah 6:9–10)

The statement is not against the healing of humanity, which is the whole purpose behind all of God's activity on earth. It is rather a caution against opening our eyes too soon, against an over-hasty entry into the spiritual realm or into states of consciousness that we need to grow into slowly and gradually. Mixing earthly and heavenly forms of vision causes uncertainty, delusions, even madness. As a result of the Fall, which was itself a premature grasping after knowledge, human beings were pushed precipitously toward becoming isolated egos in the sense world, separated from their heavenly origins and true divine parent. The divine plan to heal humanity involves holding human beings back in certain ways until the proper balance between their bodily and spiritual nature can be restored. For the same reason, a patient who has undergone an eye operation may have to remain in a dark room with their eyes bandaged for a while. Their eyes have to heal before they can be opened.

Blind people have their own ways of seeing, and sometimes restoring their sight can create problems. The neurologist Oliver Sacks tells the story of a man who was pushed by his fiancée into having an eye operation that partially restored his vision, but also left him confused and miserable. He had grown accustomed to 'seeing' things through his other senses, like touch and taste, and he was not able to re-train his brain to incorporate the visual signals he was now receiving. The incredibly complex process of eye–brain coordination is performed in early childhood when the brain is at its most malleable, and is difficult or even impossible to accomplish later in life. The man ended up closing his eyes most of the time so that he could 'see' better.[2]

The passage from Isaiah about seeing and hearing has already been quoted in connection with the parables. When the disciples ask Jesus why he uses such metaphorical stories rather than speaking plainly to the people, he replies: 'This is why I speak to them in parables, because seeing they do not see, and hearing they do not hear, nor do they understand' (Matthew 13:13). The stream of evolution that comes from the past is still leading humanity down into the world of sensory perception; human beings are not yet ready for higher understanding. This is not a value judgment, but an acknowledgment of what can best serve them. People need time to slowly train their higher faculties through imaginative pictures given to them in the form of stories about sense-perceptible things and events. Such stories, when they are spiritually true, work on a deep level without our needing to take them apart and analyze them – a death-dealing process that takes much inner strength to navigate. True stories are food for the soul on many levels, bringing us knowledge that can work in us inwardly until we are ready to understand it.

The disciples, at the forefront of human development, should have reached this next level. As Christ says to them:

> But blessed are your eyes, for they see, and your ears, for they hear. For truly, I say to you, many prophets and righteous

people longed to see what you see, and did not see it, and to hear what you hear, and did not hear it. (Matthew 13:16–17)

Though the disciples are able to understand parables when they are explained, they still have a hard time navigating more subtle shifts between the metaphorical and literal levels, between spirit and sense. This is a problem, because the point of their training is for them to behold a deed that bridges and transforms these distinctions: the crucifixion and resurrection of Christ Jesus. Already in the healing of the deaf man, we saw Jesus 'look upward' (*anablepo*). Now it is the human being who must learn to look upward once more. Will the disciples learn this higher seeing through the lessons Christ Jesus continues to enact before them?

In Mark's story of the blind man of Bethsaida, Jesus leads the man away from the crowd. As with the deaf man, these sensory healings require solitude, intimacy, and quiet. Jesus again applies his spittle, laying his hands on the man's eyes. As Rudolf Frieling points out, it is significant that two forms of the word for 'eye' are used in this passage. In this first stage, the word *omma* is used. This is a poetic term, and the man sees in a 'poetic' or 'metaphorical' way: he says he sees people walking around who look like trees. This is a truth that incorporates a vision of the life forces, which people once saw with naturally clairvoyant vision. But that time is now past. The man needs to come down further into the sense world and to see things in a more 'prosaic', more ordinary way, before he can more on to a new form of higher seeing.[3]

Jesus touches the man's eyes again, and this time the word used is the prosaic *ophthalmos*. Now the man can see without the interference of dreamlike visionary experiences. Frieling notes that three different prepositions are also used in the course of this healing. First the man 'looks up', seeing the men like trees, a vision of the life forces that surround their physical forms; then after the second laying on of hands, he 'sees through', reaching the sense-perceptible objects, and finally, he 'looks into' and sees clearly.[4]

Our descent from the spirit into the sense world is what gives us our freedom and independence, and we can then raise that to a higher level through reacquiring spiritual vision. But we must relinquish illogical fantasy, dreaminess and all the remnants of old clairvoyant vision, which will only interfere with the new organs we are meant to be forming.

Seeing and hearing are central to the path of initiation, which requires that the candidates awaken spiritual senses. Otherwise, they remain deaf and blind in that higher world. As all of humanity is now crossing the threshold, if we do not learn to look upward to heaven and open ourselves to hearing the spiritual Word, we will lose our ability to grow and evolve as we should. 'All things transitory are but a parable', says Goethe.[5] The danger is that we will become trapped in this parable if we don't learn to 'see through' it, stuck in a sense-perceptible world which, bereft of its higher meaning, becomes only a parody of reality.

We might think that such an urgent development should take place as fast as possible, but hurry and impatience are deeply harmful in this realm. 'Hasten slowly' must be our motto. Fortunately, Christ bears the knowledge of the right time and pace for each one of us to develop, and with him as our guide, we will never be pushed too far or held back too long. Trust in his guidance is our essential protection on a perilous way.

Personal Connections – Part 12

Most people I have met in my life have not been as open, as honest or as trusting as the residents of Carrefour, nor have they been as endlessly forgiving. They have said things they didn't mean, and didn't say what they really thought; they have concealed their true motives and opinions from those they did not trust. Sometimes they pushed their ideas upon others, insisting that their way was the 'right' way, or else they kept up a passive-aggressive silence. Even when they meant well and made an effort to be kind, this way of thinking and behaving cropped up, revealing a tendency to judge others and react defensively when they felt threatened.

In other words, they were 'normal' – what we would call 'only human'.

I did all of those things too, of course. But with another example of how to be human now in front of me, I started to question what the definition of that term really was. The 'norm' from which our so-called 'disabled' residents deviated was in many ways completely toxic and sick, with its undercurrent of blame, judgment and dishonesty. That might have been considered normal, but it was certainly not healthy.

The greater the capacity for intellectual thought our residents had, the more like us they were: more able to lie, dissemble and pretend. The less capable ones were not like this. And what the world might call a lack of intelligence, I came to see as a sign of wisdom. The residents were whole, in that they showed who they were without hiding anything.

That didn't mean that we, the coworkers, could necessarily understand what we were seeing. I began to think that our vaunted intellectual capabilities actually formed a kind of shield, getting in the way of more fundamental capacities for perception, feeling and comprehension. Our brain's frontal lobes, which we need for higher cognition and language, may actually wall us off from a deeper, more embodied wisdom. In many ways, the seat of our intelligence is the stupidest part of us. It allows us to do all sorts of things that go against our own best interests, against our true health and well-being.

And yet we can't simply turn off this part of our brains. We have to work our way through our blindness and stupidity into a new way of seeing and knowing, toward a moral vision that rejoins what the intellect has sundered.

The shield in our heads allows us to believe that our thoughts and feelings can't be sensed by others. The residents put an end to that delusion for me. Clearly they were affected by my inner thoughts and feelings as much as by my outer deeds and words. With them, I couldn't be divided in my consciousness, saying one thing and meaning another. If I wanted to speak to them, I had to speak with my whole being, bringing intention, feeling and will together as one. Things I did not even know about myself were often expressed, through their pure, selfless mirroring of me and everything else in their environment.

When Colleen went into one of her sulky spells, for example, I had to tell her she was safe and cared for, and really mean it. I'd never felt secure in my ability to care for anyone, and yet necessity pulled this conviction out of me. If I tried to assert anything that wasn't true, it quickly became apparent.

In my crisis with Michael, too, I was being challenged to look at things differently and to rise to another level of truth. I could see so clearly what was wrong with him and what he needed, yet he was unable to see it for himself. When I told him, he felt threatened and repulsed my efforts. This in turn ruptured my self-image and prompted me to justify and defend my position. Meanwhile, there were my own long-denied sources of dysfunction, to which I'd adapted so thoroughly that they felt like part of me, so that when they were pointed out to me by anyone, I felt wounded to my core.

It was the beam and splinter in action, and on some level I knew that. I knew that I had to work on my own self and not tell others what to do. But it was incredibly hard to actually do it.

Michael eventually agreed to have marriage counseling, but after a couple of sessions I could tell it was no use. Michael covered up his depression in public, as usual, and insisted I was overreacting. The counselor appeared unable to see through this ploy, and merely listened and nodded his head sagely, taking everything that was said at face value.

I was then inspired to suggest a different way for our counseling sessions: simply taking turns sharing our biographies. I thought this would help Michael open up about his early trauma; I didn't expect it to unearth or trigger anything in me. But when I got to the point of describing my first sexual encounter and the mind–body split I experienced then, I was shaken. I had thought I was over all of that, yet the memory could still move me to tears and stifle my words. Some mysterious, unpenetrated thing still had power over me, and I could not rationalize it away.

Michael was moved, too. In the midst of our battling, a spark of compassion awoke in him.

'I wish I had been there,' he said. 'I could have helped you.'

I didn't know how to tell him that he couldn't. The terrible split in me had nothing to do with my partner, but with something in myself, and that something was still there no matter what I told myself or others. Michael was not the only one who needed help; I did, too, and in some way that I could not yet quite grasp. But at least we were starting to make progress, even if it was slow and I frequently lost heart.

Another time, following a complete breakdown in verbal understanding, I decided to quit all my nagging and try a different tactic. I suggested that we silently rub each other's feet at night before bed, then share something from our day with no commentary or discussion, and finally say something positive about the other person. I didn't tell Michael that I had also started to pray for him, every morning and evening, doing the exercises I'd learned at Alcyon and saying verses suggested to me by friends and Christian Community priests that I'd consulted.

We did this for a while, and the results were amazing. Michael started to say he felt like he was waking up and recovering a lost part of himself. Wholeness seemed in reach for the first time.

But I was impatient. I started to push again and Michael accused me of overstepping my boundaries. Infuriated by his nasty tone, I said he could go to hell. It seemed that the positive feeling we had been nurturing between us had been irrevocably damaged.

In the days that followed, as I looked back over my life with Michael, I saw that being the only person with whom he shared his deepest emotions, including his negative ones, had once made me feel special. I had been proud to be honored with his confidence. It filled a great desire in me to be needed and worthwhile. But now, as his negative feelings grew ever stronger, and he continued to refuse to share them with anyone else, even his closest friend, I was beginning to find the burden intolerable.

I decided that I really did have to let go. Let him go to hell! Let him remain stuck in that dark, horrible, hopeless place. It wasn't that I wanted that fate for him, or that I would ever stop caring, but I had to somehow undo the subconscious bonds that kept us tied to each other, releasing what was not mine to manage and control. I didn't want to abandon him, but I had to let down my pride and admit that there was something I simply was not strong enough to bear.

I decided to create a symbol of this resolution. I took a stone that I'd brought back from our travels in Switzerland, a chunk of granite with some quartz and mica glinting within. I covered this with clay dug out from our nearby stream, and I let it dry. Here was a chunk of darkness which yet contained a hidden light, wrapped in a protective outer shell.

On June 24, the day of St. John the Baptist, I took this stone to the stream and dropped it in. I prayed that I would be able to let go of Michael's darkness, to set him free, and that the waters of life would slowly wash over it and somehow bring healing to him. I had to let go of this burden, for it was weighing me down and I could do nothing about it.

I had to give up a kind of vision, my vision of who Michael could be, what he needed, how he could be saved, in acknowledgment of my own weakness and brokenness. I had to place both of us in the hands of a higher wisdom, one that knew what we needed for our healing and salvation, as I did not. I had to walk in blindness, trusting something I could not yet see.

I didn't know if I would ever be able to 'look upward' again. I could only stumble forward, in doubt and in hope, waiting for the touch of divine grace to open my eyes.

> *Meditation*
>
> Do you see anything?

13.
A Boy with Seizures:
Mark 9:14–29

Coming Down from the Mountain

The Demons

                                      drag him

                      push him

                                  shatter him

           crush him

                                  don't let him breathe

    give him no rest

                                      he is mine!

he is mine!

                                we will smother

          and rend him

                                bruise him

            and bend him

in his death
is our life
his despair
our hope
we will never cease
till he is ours

The Boy

Oh Father
help me!
Save me!
I cannot
stand
I cannot
speak
stop

no

I

The Disciples

We did all he taught us.
We studied,
we prayed.
We carried no purse,
shook the dust off our sandals.
We have been good disciples.

The demons obeyed us!
But this —
this mad whirling
torrential volcano
this vast crowd of nothing
undoing creation
vacant
and bursting
howling
and silent —
How can we oppose it?
We are but mortal…

The Father

Helpless
and ashamed
I behold my boy,
my seed
barely sprouted
cut off at the root,
my weakness
made plain
for all to see.
For I too turn to flame,
I too fall and drown.
In my secret heart
I am no more whole
than this tortured child
who but plays out my pain.

Agonies of doubt and fear,
pulling me down a bottomless well;
terrible waves of righteousness
firing me with deadly power.
As his mouth fills with foam
as he writhes and rolls
so do I,
so do I…

And when these have passed
the husk of me sags
powerless
empty
silent
alone
forsaken
abandoned
rejected by God.

But here –
one comes
as a seed of power
not yet spent
not wasted
but stored up for us
to save us
to seed us
to give us

the strength
to stand
the will
to believe
the courage
to speak…

O Lord
help and save!
My faith
so weak –
let me be consumed
by your radiant love
or buried with you
in a bottomless tomb

only

take my seed
let it die
and bear
let it live
let us shine

let him rise

Reflections on *A Boy with Seizures*

The healing of a boy with seizures is the climax of the whole series of healings in the Synoptic Gospels. It directly follows the event known as the Transfiguration, which in the Gospel of Mark forms the exact center of the narrative, its crucial turning point.[1]

Jesus had begun to speak to the disciples of his death and resurrection, but they were not able to take in this momentous thought, as shown by Peter immediately rebuking him. Still, Jesus continued to teach the counterintuitive wisdom they would need in order to pass through the coming death-experience: 'For whoever would save his life will lose it, but whoever loses his life for my sake and the gospel's will save it' (Mark 8:35).

Six days later, upon a mountain, three of his closest disciples saw Jesus transfigured, radiating light and speaking with Moses and Elijah. Peter wanted to make tabernacles for the three figures, to shelter and contain them, symbolic of preserving past tradition. But a cloud obscured the disciples' vision, and they heard a voice telling them to listen to 'my beloved son'. When the cloud cleared they saw only Jesus in his earthly aspect.

In the gospels, going up a mountain refers to a raising of consciousness, not necessarily to a physical location. Traditionally, however, the mountain has been identified as Mount Tabor, which is located in the middle of Galilee not far from Nain, where the widow's son was raised. Rising abruptly from its flat surroundings, the isolated mountain's dome-like appearance strongly recalls the shape of the human head, and thus resonates with the place of the skull: Golgotha. At the foot of the mountain is an important intersection of trade routes leading east and west, south and north. The crossroads that humanity has reached in its development is indicated in anticipation of the crucifixion.

But the disciples are wrestling with the impossibility of that predicted event. How can the savior of humanity be killed on a cross, a humiliation reserved for the worst criminals? How can the quest to heal and restore Israel be achieved by the Son of Man dying?

Even as they progress further on their path of knowledge, the survival instinct is still warring inside them with the new principle of total self-giving that is to be born on Golgotha. Inevitably, growing insight into the spirit is attended by a strengthening of the forces that oppose higher human development, as is indicated in Jesus's rebuke of Peter: 'Get behind me, Satan' (Mark 8:33). Yes, even his own most intimate student could become the vessel of evil. But the healing that follows demonstrates the remedy.

Coming down from the mountain, the group meets the other disciples, who are surrounded by a great crowd and arguing with scribes. When Jesus asks what they are arguing about, a man appears with his son, who suffers from seizures. The disciples have been unable to heal him. The father says the boy is possessed by a spirit that makes him mute, throws him to the ground and makes him rigid, and often casts him into fire and into water to destroy him. He has been like this from childhood.

The forces of evil that confront humanity are of two natures and have been called by various names. Rudolf Steiner calls them Lucifer and Ahriman and has greatly enlarged our understanding of these beings. Both of them, it is important to emphasize, have brought great gifts: Lucifer in the form of artistic and cultural inspiration, and Ahriman by connecting us to the earthly world and all the scientific and technical expertise that we can develop here. The two sides must be kept in balance, however, or they become destructive. They throw us into the fire of delusional, egotistic feeling, or they drown us in materialism, severing our connection to the spirit.

This is the dual danger faced by evolving humanity: the higher self in us has not yet matured sufficiently to resist such overwhelming forces. Our ordinary, everyday self has to come to an awareness of the need for help, and open itself to the good forces that alone can bring us the power we need to overcome evil. A step in humility and faith is required: 'All things are possible for one who believes,' says Jesus (Mark 9:23). The word translated here as 'possible' is *dunatos*. It does not refer to an abstract, theoretical sort of possibility; rather it denotes power, strength, might. Power comes into the one who has trust in the Good. With all the confusion of spiritual powers at work around and within us, discerning which power to trust in is the tricky part.

When danger threatens in the physical world, our ego instinctively seeks to bolster and protect itself, exerting its control in order to survive. But when the threats come from spiritual powers, that control must be loosened, for otherwise the good forces cannot come close to us. We must risk letting go completely, retaining only our faith that we will not be abandoned by divine love.

To the question of why the disciples were not able to heal the boy, Jesus responds that this kind of spirit cannot be driven out by anything but prayer. But who prays in this story? Surely, it is the boy's father. In crying out, 'I believe; help my unbelief,' he expresses both his recognition of the divine Helper, and his experience of the evil forces that are also active within him. He relinquishes the illusion that by his self-willed striving alone he can overcome evil. He comes to the crux of the paradox: in order to be saved, one has to be willing to die.

The disciples were not able to die the death of the ego that wants to stay in control and secure its own salvation. Even the closest followers of Christ Jesus are prone to this danger, which potentially makes them the most dangerous of all: if they do not see their own need for help, they can do great harm.

Jesus commands the mute and deaf spirit to release the boy, saying 'Come out of him and never enter him again.' The adversarial spirits want to rob us of our true voice. They keep us silent, unable even to think our real thoughts or feel our real feelings, deaf to the inner word of truth. Those who have suffered trauma know this experience, and know how hard and yet how necessary the path toward recovering one's own mind and soul is. As Bessel van der Kolk puts it, healing involves coming to 'know what you know and feel what you feel'.[2] The result is a new experience of life. For those who overcome trauma, it can seem that for the first time they can truly live in their own body.

In the story, the boy appears 'like a corpse' once the spirit comes out of him. But Jesus takes him by the hand and raises him up – an image that anticipates the resurrection.

Christ Jesus does not directly work upon the disciples as a healer, but leaves a space open in which they can choose to take up that path, having witnessed the sequence of healing deeds that culminates here. Finding healing oneself is the essential first step to healing others, for otherwise we will merely pass on our own illness in the course of trying to 'help'. This is one way to understand what it means to remove the beam from our own eye before attempting to remove the splinter from our neighbor's eye. As we saw with the first healing of the demon-possessed man, there must be a process of catharsis in which we work through past experiences that trouble our souls and disturb our physical health.

But completely eliminating weak points is neither possible nor desirable. The mystery of humanity is actually connected to our powerlessness, out of which a strength is born that we did not know we had until we were pushed to the breaking point.[3] The pride that can attend spiritual achievement must be turned to humility, to poverty of spirit, before the true human potential can be realized.

The higher beings who seek to teach us and lead us onward surround us with all kinds of learning aids, images, stories, and experiences that would lead us in the right direction. Yet we are also surrounded by false and misleading messages originating from forces inimical to humanity. This is essential, for how could we be free if we were embedded in goodness without consciousness or choice? Our freedom awakens when the core of goodness and truth in us recognizes its own likeness in what appears as if from the outside, and distinguishes it from what is evil and false.

Christ's healing of this boy represents his promise that if we turn to him and trust in him, the adversarial powers will no longer be able to overwhelm us, even if we experience a deathlike nullification of egoistic control. Christ's resurrection is the seed of our own resurrection. With this healing, he shows the disciples, and us, the purpose for which he came to earth. In our own time, when we lift the clouds that fog our thinking, open our hearts to authentic feeling, and turn our wills toward making manifest all that is good and true, we will be able to see him walking with us. Faith and trust in that presence provides the solid ground we need while we develop the higher knowing that is still only in its germinal stages.

Personal Connections – Part 13

Increasingly, I was struck by the multiple faces Michael could wear. There was 'Nice Michael', the people-pleasing public persona that was attractive but false; and 'Mean Michael', the one who hurt me with his critical, judgmental attitude. I was sure that neither of these were good for 'Real Michael', the person I knew from our intimate encounters, the one I loved and trusted.

Michael refused to acknowledge there was a problem, but under the stress of our conflict his 'Nice Michael' mask was starting to slip. People in the community began to notice, but when they called him out on it he only became more scared and defensive. Because no one else was allowed to see the other side of him, I was the recipient of those feelings.

While I was at the mindfulness retreat at Alcyon, away from the habits of thought and behavior that bound me in everyday life, I'd been able to fully acknowledge and articulate at last that the way 'Mean Michael' treated me was not right, and I was not to blame for it. And yet, I still felt that I bore some responsibility for changing the dynamic between us. I believed that Michael's hurtful behavior was not coming from his true self; some unhealed, unacknowledged injury was causing him to act this way, as well as causing his need to pretend to be stronger than he really was. And once, I had been glad to lean on the strength of his warm, caring side to make me feel better about myself. Then I'd shut down when he hurt me, without even wondering what hurt of his own might lie behind that.

Clearly, we both needed support to help us communicate better about our painful feelings, without withdrawing from each other when things got rough. I really wanted to change that pattern now, but I couldn't do it by myself. We seemed to be at an impasse.

After my resolution to leave Michael's 'dark side' alone, we didn't talk about it for some weeks. Then, following another of my tearful outbursts, he surprised me by saying that he couldn't see what I was so upset about or why I thought he needed help, and he wanted to understand. He seemed genuine and sincere about this.

Had my letting go led to some positive development after all?

I wanted to explain myself, but I decided to hold back. I knew I needed a witness for such a conversation, and so I said I would tell him in the presence of our marriage counselor the following week.

It was hard to wait, but I held back any impulse to talk about my worries as I struggled to cope with my tasks at home and work. For his part, after some people told him his behavior was making them uncomfortable, Michael was growing increasingly anxious about his reputation and job security. He was starting to criticize and blame me again. Under these circumstances, how could I most effectively use our upcoming meeting?

The day before, I spoke to a priest I'd been going to regularly for spiritual direction to talk about what I should say. I'd been going over various scenarios in my head, trying to find the best way to make Michael understand. The priest cautioned me that I could not tell an adult what to do. I realized that in spite of my intentions and my symbolic stone-in-the-water ritual, I was still wanting to manage and control the situation, to direct it in the way I thought best for everyone.

I had to stop that. I had to stop trying to make Michael do what I considered best for him. He had to figure that out for himself.

But he'd asked why I thought he needed help, and I wanted to give an answer. I decided that the best way was to simply tell my story.

In the counseling session that's what I did. I told the story of my life with Michael, how when I got together with him I was not well myself, and didn't really see him. I was just using him to serve my own needs for affection and approval. Then, when Brendan was born and Michael withdrew his affection from me, I was in shock. I still didn't see Michael and his underlying depression, nor did I care for him properly. I felt only my own pain. As a result this depression – his and mine – went underground again.

I should have spoken up at the time. I should have known that it is not good for a baby to have even one depressed parent, let alone two. But Brendan was not yet real to me then, either.

However, that had changed, and now, through our more recent crisis, I could no longer stay silent. I truly cared about Michael and wanted him to find a way out of the hell he was trapped in. I was not telling him what to do. I did not want to force him to get help. But I simply could not deny that I thought he needed help.

Sometimes, I said, I felt as though negative forces were attacking me through him. I realized that however hard that was for me, it must have been even more terrible for Michael to live with that negative energy. There had also been moments recently when I felt that something had changed. Those forces were gone, and it was just him. I could tell the difference between them and him. All I wanted was for this distinction to grow, for him to be free and able to be himself.

I was so sorry that I had not seen this or spoken up sooner; I felt responsible for letting it go on so long. Although Michael had told me more than once that I cared too much and that I should just leave him alone, I couldn't help caring. That was all I could say.

I talked for a long time, so Michael didn't have much time to respond. As soon as he did, I knew the window of openness toward me had shut down completely. In his anxiety to protect himself from any criticism, he blamed me for everything. He mocked and derided me and said things that weren't true. He said that if I had just talked to him more about his dark side, I would have understood. Except he had told me before that he didn't want to talk about it, and I had respected that!

I wanted to defend myself, but I held my tongue. As my spiritual director had advised, I struggled not to react immediately and to observe what was happening. What was coming at me from Michael?

It was anger.

In this conversation, unlike in some of our previous stormy encounters, I had tried to be calm, rational, and balanced, even as I expressed the reality of my concern for him. In explaining why I thought he needed help, I strove not to demand anything from him except that he hear me out. I tried not to blame him, and to describe how I had also been at fault.

Most people would be grateful to hear that someone cared about their welfare. I had been grateful when someone cared enough about me to tell me I needed help. His reaction was anger.

Why? Why did this make him so angry?

We had to leave, our time was up. On our way home, we needed to stop at the pharmacy to pick up a prescription. Sitting in the car in the parking lot, I asked him that question.

It was a stupid thing to do. I had resolved not to talk about these matters without a witness, but our session had left too many things unresolved. I felt compelled to open up the topic once more.

Michael's response this time was so intense that it scared me. My fear had been growing lately, because he seemed to be falling apart inwardly. Even when I tried to speak calmly about concerns that I thought were objective and not only about my own emotional reactions, his anger escalated to the point where he lost all sense of commitment to the truth. He would tell outright lies, twist my words to suit himself, belittle me, blame me for everything, and refuse to take any responsibility himself. 'There is no truth,' he had told me in one of these moods. This behavior was utterly at odds with the strong moral center that I had sensed at his core. I felt that his true inner being was completely obscured and some other element seemed to have taken over.

Such defenses did not provide a reliable source of protection, but he didn't know how to survive without them. He was no more able to listen to reason than a wounded animal.

I had had enough. I couldn't live with a person who scared me with his irrational anger, even though I still loved him. I had to admit that in my quest to help him, I had failed.

Struggling with my own anger, I got out of the car and went into the drugstore. When I came out, I sat in the back seat.

When we got home, I took the necessary steps to have Michael removed from the community. He didn't want to go, but he had no choice. 'I want Brendan!' he said. I didn't respond, knowing we'd have to deal with that later. I stood there in our kitchen, shaking but resolute. I didn't want to do this, but I knew I had to.

He had a camper van that he could sleep in while the next steps were decided. He packed a few things upstairs, came down without looking at me, got in the van, and drove off.

It was over. Our fourteen-year marriage was finished.

Or maybe not.

Two days later Michael called me. His voice was trembling; I had never heard him sound like that. He asked if there was any hope, and I said I didn't think I could live with him anymore.

He gasped in pain and said he just had to tell me that when he thought about what happened, when he saw me in his mind standing there, it was like something broke in him. He finally saw me and understood me as he never had before. Couldn't we talk? It would mean so much to him.

Was this real, or some kind of trick? I said of course we could talk, if he really wanted to, but he had to know I needed to be careful.

He knew that, and he wanted so much to be with me and Brendan, but he understood if that wasn't possible. He just hoped I would read a letter he wanted to send me.

I hung up the phone utterly amazed by this transformation. What I heard in his voice seemed real. Was there hope after all?

He was staying with a mutual friend of ours, who came to get some things for him and give me the letter. He said that Michael was going through an incredible process and they were talking a lot. I was glad, but still cautious.

In the letter Michael repeated what he had said on the phone. Here is some of what he wrote:

> I don't even know how to put this – after what was possibly the most miserable night in my life. I'm scared, really scared, that it is too late. Of course I was thinking again and again about what happened, about what you said, about what I said. And I could suddenly see your face, when you were standing there… And I could understand. I could understand your fear! And something happened, something opened up in that moment and I realized: You matter to me! You, Brendan, the three of us as a family, is what gives me grounding, what gives me purpose, what I value most. Lory – I do still love you!
>
> I know it is possibly too late, I should have realized it long ago. But I needed this shock experience to make me

understand. I did you wrong. I recognized only a part of you when we met. It took all these years to get to know you better, but I still didn't realize! Until now.

I cannot even begin to express my amazement at this. The person I had seen fall apart and collapse into a vortex of defensive untruth was standing up, taking responsibility, having empathy, valuing relationships – acquiring a conscience! It was like seeing someone who was paralyzed get up and begin to walk, or even like seeing someone who was dead come back to life.

Of course I wanted to talk to him, to see if we could get back together. If he had truly taken a step toward wholeness, if his real self had come into its rightful place in his inner kingdom, then I would not need to fear for him. Beyond all hope or expectation, had my dearest wish been granted?

In the story of the boy healed of his seizures and restored to life, I am reminded of this moment when something I never thought possible came to pass. And in the father of the boy, who expressed the painful division in himself and admitted his need for divine help to bring him back to wholeness, I can see my own earlier split and my own incapacity. There was a point beyond which my own forces could not bring me, a place of death, a wall that seemed to show no way through.

But Christ is the Door, and in the light of his transfigured being, a new way did open up for us. When I asked Michael later what had happened to him after I kicked him out, he said it had been a Christ experience. He couldn't say much more than that; it seemed to be inexpressible.

I thought I understood what he meant, though, because Christ had also brought me out from a place of anger into a place of freedom where I was able to understand and connect with people again. Knowing that we both followed the same leader enabled me to trust him again, and to take up our path together once more.

I have never been quite able to comprehend what it was that Michael saw in place of my real self, what was the obstacle obscuring his vision and causing him to misunderstand me in spite of all my efforts to communicate. But whatever it was, I can tell the difference now that the obstacle is gone. Clearly he can see and understand me to a degree that was not possible before, and that has enabled trust to be reborn between us: not just my trust in him and his promises, but my trust in my own ability to know what is real. Somehow, showing my fear and admitting my failure opened the door to that reality in a way I could never have anticipated. I still regard it with amazement, awe, and wonder.

There were still a lot of dark layers to explore, in myself most of all. At the same time, however, something had been brought up into the light, and it remained there. It was an incredible, miraculous birth.

Hallelujah.

Meditation

I have faith; help my lack of faith.

14.
A Woman with a Disabling Spirit:
Luke 13:10–17

Daughter of Abraham

It was eighteen years into Great Herod's reign
when he took it in hand to restore our Temple,
to glorify God, or at least himself –
for him the difference was small.

My father was a mason, one of a thousand,
and a priest as well, as all must be
who worked on the holy restoration,
enlarging, repairing, making whole.

It soothed him to do this, as if our people,
shattered and scattered to the ends of the earth,
could as simply be brought back and rebuilt
as stones placed one on another.

But I did not think so. Though merely a girl,
not allowed to study or preach the scriptures,
I knew by heart the ones I'd heard,
I knew the words of the promise.

Our land had been stolen, our people betrayed.
The wicked reigned, and we had no king.
The faithful were parched fields waiting for rain.
Where was the one who would come in the clouds?

When my father collapsed one day beneath
his last load of bricks and mortar, I wept
for the waste of effort, the hopeless ruin
of Israel's hope and Abraham's seed.

There was a boy who loved me, and wanted
to speak for me, but I refused him.
My mother cried and called me insane,
but I stood firm. In these last days

I did not want to carry a babe
I'd only have to fear for, and run with
into the hills when the wrath of God
finally blasted us clean.

And so I fell back to this synagogue,
awaiting the word that would turn to flame
and fire the limp hearts of my sheepish folk
into something stronger than clay.

But I heard nothing, and as the years
piled into decades, I started to bend,
to shift, to collapse, like a tumbled wall
that could no longer bear any weight.

For eighteen years I'd been so bent,
eyeing the floor of the synagogue
and listening with only half an ear
to the usual moans, when I heard him.

'Woman, you are free.' Could it truly be
the one who had come to open our prison?
His word was not as I'd expected.
No flames of wrath, no furious blast,

but a gentle thrill that entered my spine
and straightened my spirit, so that I could see
my people again, standing like pillars,
bearing the weight of the world.

Let us be his temple. Let songs of praise
resound from the ones he lifts and straightens,
building a kingdom made not with hands
but with our unfettered hearts.

Reflections on *A Woman with a Disabling Spirit*

The latter part of the Luke Gospel, following the Feeding of the Five Thousand, has a very different structure than either Matthew or Mark. While those two gospels are crammed with incidents leading up to Peter's recognition of Jesus as the bearer of the Christ-being, including Jesus walking on water, Luke jumps directly to Peter's confession. From this point the three Synoptic Gospels follow the same pattern for a while, then Luke takes a very different course before the accounts come back together again shortly before the entry into Jerusalem on Palm Sunday. Included in Luke's unique content are three healings not found anywhere else in the gospels, the first of which is that of the woman with a 'disabling spirit' who has been bent over for eighteen years.

The number eighteen is surely significant, like all numbers in the Bible, but what does it mean? When I came across the fact that Herod the Great began to restore the Temple in Jerusalem in the eighteenth year of his reign, I thought I had found a clue. Did this have something to do with the raising up of the 'daughter of Abraham'?

The term 'daughter of Abraham' indicates that the woman is a representative of her whole people, just as the 'Son of Man' is the representative of humanity. The woman's body cannot stand up straight, just as the ruined Temple in Jerusalem can no longer hold the religion of her people. The gospel accounts cannot be dated with certainty, but most scholars believe they were written at some point after the Second Temple was finally destroyed in AD 70.

In the centuries leading up to the birth of Jesus, oppression and persecution of the Jewish people under their foreign rulers gave rise to a new genre of apocalyptic literature, notably the Book of Daniel and the apocryphal Book of Enoch. The emerging idea of a Messiah, or promised redeemer, was strengthened and elaborated. The term 'Son of Man' was introduced for a human-divine figure that has power over earth and is enthroned in heaven.[1] I imagined that the woman in my poem was steeped in such images and longing for the promised release.

With the Romans' brutal quashing of the final Jewish rebellion in the first century AD, hope for a Messiah who would bring about an external rebirth of the kingdom was severely challenged. But Christ restores humanity from within, not without. Old forms have fallen and cannot be repaired, but something can still arise when we reconnect to the lasting truth that built those forms in the first place and can continue to build ever-new structures for itself.

The objection made by the 'ruler of the synagogue' to healing on the Sabbath is shown in its absurdity: 'There are six days in which work ought to be done. Come on those days and be healed, and not on the Sabbath day.' But healing is not work: it is life and regeneration; it is holiness itself. Surely healing belongs to the Lord more than any other activity?

Perhaps part of the healing function of the Sabbath was to hold something back in humanity for a time, keeping a space open until the Healer could come to earth. As we saw with the healings of the deaf and blind men, healing must happen at the right moment and cannot be rushed. But great harm can result if we keep holding back once the divine healing presence has arrived. It is indicative of an inner numbness, a lack of common-sense knowledge of what is needed for life and well-being. While Luke does not recount the healings of the deaf and blind men found in Mark, this story indicates the uprightness and freedom that true seeing and hearing gives to our spiritual selves when we consent to the divine plan and return to the right stream of development.

The word translated as 'disabling' is *asthenia*, 'weakness', the same word used in the case of the man at the pool of Bethesda in the Gospel of John. The woman is weak, worn out like the ritual practices of her people that need to be constructed anew to fit the stream of future evolution. Christ Jesus sees her, calls her over to him, and speaks the word of freedom from bondage (*apoluo*) that also means forgiveness of sins. He touches her with his hands and at once she is restored to uprightness (*anorthoo*). This same word is used by the author of Luke in the book of Acts, which quotes the prophet Amos:

> After this I will return, and I will rebuild the tent of David that has fallen; I will rebuild its ruins, and I will restore [*anorthoo*] it, that the remnant of mankind may seek the Lord, and all the Gentiles who are called by my name, says the Lord, who makes these things known from of old. (Acts 15:16–18)

This rebuilding is also an undoing of something that has been diverted onto a wrong path. It restores an original condition of uprightness that the human being has been lacking since the Fall. Christ Jesus shows us, through his whole way of being, the rebuilt, rightly constructed human Temple. When we are seen by him, when we hear his call to freedom and feel his touch upon us, we become the people of God we were meant to be.

Personal Connections – Part 14

A year after the miraculous rebirth of our family, we were living in Switzerland, where Michael had found another job. He moved in February, and Brendan and I followed in June after finishing out the school year.

It was a huge transition to make, but we couldn't stay where we were. In fact, I realized that Michael and I should never have taken on the job as house-parents when there was so much still to work through in our personal relationship. The challenge of such an intensely interconnected work–life situation had brought many long-hidden things to light, and while this was good, it proved too much for us to handle. Our marriage and our individual psychic health had to be re-established on a firmer basis, and to do that we needed to be free of such a heavy responsibility for other people.

Our departure from the community left many things unresolved, which was hard for me. I tried to keep in mind that the residents didn't judge me; rather they saw me and accepted me for who I was. I could never pay back what I owed them, or make up for the mistakes I'd made, but I could learn to live according to their example by growing in empathy, compassion, forgiveness and trust.

I continued to attend the communion service of the Christian Community whenever I could, and although I often found it difficult to follow, I knew that whatever effort I made brought me closer to a place of calm and inner strength. I kept doing the inner practices that I'd learned, and experimented with mindfulness meditation and centering prayer. I trusted that these practices were having an effect even if I didn't consciously experience it all the time.

When we arrived in Switzerland, though, my body seemed to fall apart. I'd already been dealing with perimenopausal symptoms that included heavy bleeding, along with the migraines and digestive issues that had never gone away. During the most intense months of crisis I barely slept. I paced the house and the streets at night, crying uncontrollably and feeling on the edge of a breakdown. Although Michael and I had reconciled, I could not immediately trust the change in him, and so we had lived apart for almost a year. This gave me the added stress of single parenting and managing an international move by myself. Now, jobless and uncertain how I'd cope in a country where I didn't speak the language, I found myself flooded with congestion, sneezing as if with an allergic reaction. I'd never had seasonal allergies before; had I suddenly developed them now? Was I allergic to Switzerland? Or was this a new menopause symptom?

I looked up 'menopause allergies' and found out about histamine intolerance, which does affect many menopausal women. A restricted diet and eliminating toxins was the recommended way to deal with it, so I started to experiment with that. I'd tried tweaking my diet in the past to see if it would help my headaches, but never anything so radical as this: the list of foods I'd have to give up was discouragingly long. However, I needed to do something because my body was clearly not well. For a long time I'd been holding myself together in public and ignoring or denying what lurked beneath the surface, but with so many of my familiar supports removed, I could no longer stay in that state of denial.

Then the COVID pandemic hit and the entire world fell apart. All kinds of inner and outer structures seemed to be collapsing, while restrictive controls were put in place to prop up a fragile sense of security. Some people rebelled against those controls, asserting their personal freedom, which made others angry at the 'antisocial' behavior that threatened their own safety. There was so much fear and uncertainty, made worse by people who clung rigidly to their opinion as though it were incontrovertible truth and lashed out at anyone who questioned it.

It was like an autoimmune disease of humanity, with various cells unable to recognize others as part of the same organism, and fighting against them. As I wrestled with my own autoimmune condition, I saw that the same battle raged within me, with various parts opposing, restricting, or attacking other parts. How could I come to know a higher organizing principle that would bring peace to my warring elements?

Over the two years of the pandemic, as I slowly found a new foothold in another country, I also researched how I could be more healthy in my body and soul. Inwardly I was still shaky, still subject to attacks of rage and sadness, and I knew now that it was too much to expect Michael to be my sole emotional support. I sought out counseling and sacramental consultation. Fortunately, since I was not yet fluent enough in French or German, I was able to find helpers who spoke English to help me in such conversations.

When I brought my symptoms to my new doctor, he ordered a battery of tests, including an ultrasound which revealed I had a large gallstone obstructing my gallbladder. He prescribed immediate surgery, but I wanted to wait and see if the changes I'd started to make in my diet and lifestyle could help. I didn't believe the conventional view that the gallbladder is an unnecessary and dispensable organ, for surely all organs in the body are important. Even though surgery might prove to be necessary, I didn't want to discard an organ I'd never given a thought to without at least understanding what might have contributed to its dysfunction. Perhaps I could reverse that.

The collapse of my former life was disturbing, but it proved to be a gift. Now that I had shed the unhealthy habit of never wanting to reveal my weakness or ask for help, new possibilities opened up. Michael was no longer resistant to admitting his own need for help, and was able to reach out and find his own supports. Our marriage could become the source of strength and comfort it was meant to be, based on mutual respect and honoring each other's individual integrity.

Like the 'daughter of Abraham' whose bodily temple had been destroyed, I found that something was calling to me to lift up my head amidst the rubble. We humans are weak, fragile creatures in so many ways. And yet, there is a vein of spiritual strength within each one of us that can bear us through all crises and obstacles if only we are able to connect with it. Just as the spine has freed itself from the bonds of gravity to point toward the stars, this spiritual essence can become straight and true once more, in cooperation with the one who upholds the archetype from which we fall again and again. With renewed determination, I set out on that path.

> *Meditation*
> You are freed from your weakness.

15.

A Man with Dropsy:

Luke 14:1–6

What Is Lawful

We were gathered, as usual, on the Sabbath,
eating cold meat and speaking hot words.
A feast of complaint, of disbelief
at the sorry pass our nation had come to.
Here we were, the chosen people,
the light meant to outshine all other men,
now chained like a dog, licking the hand
of the master who starved and beat us.
And there they were, those sleepwalkers,
mumbling their rituals in a room
that had a long time been empty.
There, blood was but blood,
bread only bread.
The inviolate space
had been entered.

What mattered now was the quickening Word,
the fire in the mind that passed between us
as we sat at table, remembering
the greatness we had been gifted.
It flared to life in our communion.
The Law was alive, a new creation
that would bring us again God's favor and love
and keep us free within our bonds.
It went to my head like good strong wine,
and my spirit soared
as it filled my veins.

But my body betrayed me.
It too filled up,
swelled, overflowed,
not with God's loving grace
like David's cup,
but with pressure and pain.
The talk still flowed around my head
but I sat in silence
and tried not to burst.

Then I saw him looking at me –
that man, the odd one, the wandering healer
who paid small heed to our Sabbath laws.
Why was he here? Who had invited
this blatant transgressor to our feast?
The others stopped talking and looked at him.

All their words dried up
to one silent question:
What will he do?
Will he break the law?
Will he give us cause
to condemn and kill?

He asked of us
to open our hearts, to dare to be healed
of the emptiness of our Godless minds,
of the terror we covered up with talk,
of the anguish that filled our loneliness.

It was no longer needed.
The Light had come.
Now, would we follow his Way?
Would we make the ritual real again,
not in a building, a space of stone,
but in the spaciousness of our lives,
the sacrifice of our hardened selves?

The others were silent, and so was I.
My mind held still, my mouth was frozen,
unable to shout a joyful 'Yes!'
It had been filled up
so long with lies.

But my body replied
with the word of truth.
I felt my release,
the pressure relaxed,
the fluid gone.
I was free to move,
free to go –
to live
unchained by fear,
fulfilled with light,
obeying one teaching:
Love.

Reflections on *A Man with Dropsy*

The healing of a man with dropsy – known today as edema – is one of three interspersed among Christ's essential teachings leading up to the Crucifixion in the latter part of Luke's Gospel. Jesus has been invited to eat at the house of a prominent Pharisee on the Sabbath, when it is unlawful for Jews to do any work. When the man suffering from edema appears in front of Jesus, everyone waits and watches closely to see what he will do. Jesus turns to the Pharisees and the experts on the law and asks: 'Is it lawful to heal on the Sabbath, or not?' Faced with this direct challenge, they remain silent.

The Pharisees were one of several groups that developed within Judaism during the Second Temple period (586 BC–AD 70). They were a progressive and relatively democratic movement, who were struggling to move with the times and adapt to the immense changes that had confronted the Jewish religion. The discussion and debate of the Torah, its meaning and application to life outside the Temple, was the center of the Pharisees' religious activity. They applied the law in ways that other groups within Judaism did not. For example, the Pharisees said that all Jews must observe the purity rules that in the written Torah applied only in the context of Temple worship. In its extreme form, this thinking held that the Temple worship had been invalidated by the first desecration of the holy space, which had been sacked by the Egyptians and Assyrians and then destroyed by the Babylonians in 586 BC. After this supremely traumatic event, the Pharisees maintained, the Temple could not truly be restored.

Out of this stream grew the rabbinic form of Judaism. Its creative task was to transform the ritual worship that no longer had a body, a Temple, in which to live, into a more inner, more individually active and living form. The Pharisees therefore had much in common with those who followed the way of Christ. But although there were some who were sympathetic to Jesus and became his disciples (most notably Nicodemus in the Gospel of John), others were hostile and felt threatened by this alternate source of progressive change.

In his depiction of a Sabbath gathering of Pharisees, Luke is surely making a reference to such a community of innovative thinkers and debaters, stirred up and inspired by their verbal wrestlings with the word of God. It must have been an exciting, but somewhat dangerous activity: any departure from divinely ordered rules and rituals involves the risk of self-inflation and ungrounded, inflammatory thinking. That seemed to me to be also connected with the diagnosis of edema in this healing, for edema is a swelling of bodily tissues caused by extra fluid leaking from the capillaries. It can be caused by sitting too long and eating too much salty food, such as at a banquet, for example. Drinking alcohol can also cause fluid retention.

It is a great temptation in our own time, with our incredible capacity for intellectual thinking, to become caught up in the flow of debate. As a result we lose touch with the silent heart-forces that keep us connected to the true source of life. Our thoughts, surging around in our heads, distance us from our bodies and immobilize our higher spiritual faculties. It is because of this that the Pharisees are unable to answer Jesus's question.

Jesus heals the man and sends him away. Here the Greek word *apoluo* is used, the same word that was used with the woman who was bent over. Its primary meaning is release from bondage. Connection with the living truth releases us from the chains we ourselves form through an intellectualism divorced from reality. It pulls us out of the hole we can dig for ourselves through the very activities we consider most sacred and holy.

This is not to say that the continued practice of Judaism is wrong.

There is no one religion or philosophical framework that has a monopoly upon insight into the laws of life and healing. Any system of thought can become rigid and lose sight of what is truly important; Christianity is highly prone to the same danger, and needs just as much of a reorientation and renewal in our time as did the Pharisees Jesus met at the feast.

Writer and doctor Rachel Naomi Remen tells a story about a child in her oncology practice who was brought for treatments by her father, an Orthodox rabbi. One of the girl's treatments fell on Yom Kippur, the holiest of holy days, when travel by car is strictly forbidden. The father said he could not bring his daughter on that day, but Dr Remen told him the treatment was vital. He said he would ask his own rabbi, his revered teacher.

On the day in question, the father and daughter were there. Dr Remen asked what the man's rabbi had said. The father replied that his teacher had instructed him to bring his daughter for treatment in a taxi, so that she might know that even a rabbi could ride on the holiest of days for the purpose of preserving life. The most important thing was that she 'not feel separated from God by this breaking of the law'.[1]

Can true healing ever be unlawful? Is there any time during which it should not be permitted? We might want to take a pause from our feast of words, fill our mind with that question, and contemplate it in silence. It may lead to our release from much that is currently holding us in bondage.

Personal Connections – Part 15

In Switzerland, I was hired for a part-time position within the organization where Michael had gotten a full-time job. We were both caring for adults with developmental disabilities again, although as it's not a live-in community, we had our own separate apartment. I was lucky to get this job. Before moving here, I had no idea how strict the Swiss are about paperwork and qualifications. You need a qualification to do everything, even cleaning houses and babysitting. For the kind of language-oriented work I was used to doing, like editing and publicity, you would need advanced language skills in French and German that I do not have.

After a few months of feeling like a babbling fool, and wanting to increase our income, I had a brainwave: I could teach English! I signed up for a course that would give me a basic qualification to teach adults in private lessons or schools.

Teaching was one of those areas where I'd always felt hampered. Ever since my master's degree program, one of my recurring nightmares had been being in front of a class of children who were going out of control. The chaos would spiral around me, and I would be helpless to do anything about it.

These dreams continued as I had my own child and experienced similar moments of helplessness. They started to ease only after I'd been working with developmentally disabled individuals for a few years, which gave me the chance to practice teaching in an entirely different context. I had to teach our volunteers not academic skills, but skills for living and for caring, skills that I learned myself in the process of teaching them. I also had opportunities to teach the residents through living with them and caring for them, as well as in a more traditional role: teaching small group classes in eurythmy, puppetry, poetry-writing, history. I started to regain the confidence in myself as a teacher that had been destroyed by the blackouts and the nerves and the anger attacks.

At festival celebrations, someone usually gave a brief talk to highlight some aspect of the season and its meaning. I started to volunteer for this and found that I really loved doing it. At first I was nervous speaking to such a large group, but I didn't black out. Instead, as I looked around the room at those dear faces, I grew calmer. Some in the circle were nodding and smiling warmly, others frowning, or looking sleepy or blank, but it didn't matter what their outer appearance might be. I knew that none of them were criticizing me or thinking how foolish I was, and that enabled me to relax and stay in my body. I was able to think clearly, sharing the thoughts that came to me about our beautiful earth and the spirit that allowed us to live in it together.

My students might not be able to do very much in worldly terms, but doing what they could do invariably gave them joy. And this joy was the healing balm for my fear and uncertainty. There was no one sitting in judgment over me or deciding I wasn't good enough. There was only one goal: to live as joyfully and as peacefully as possible.

There was no mandate to live *quickly*. That had been the drive of my own schooling, but I was learning how to slow down now, and finding it an immense relief.

When it came time to teach the students in my English certificate course, I found that I enjoyed preparing and teaching my lessons, even the ones that went awry. I didn't feel crushed by feedback from my supervisors, but was able to take it in and use it to improve my next lesson.

I enjoyed helping students communicate better, but the challenge of teaching English was much greater than I had ever expected. That's because speaking a language from birth and being able to teach it are two entirely different things. In fact, teaching one's mother tongue means stepping outside of the body you were born in, and looking at it from the outside. It means assessing something consciously that you would otherwise take completely for granted, and trying to figure out how to build it up from the very beginning. It's a good thing to do, and yet disorienting. I'm not sure I would have plunged into it if I'd understood what it involved – as with so many other decisions in my life.

And yet I'm grateful for this challenge. When I first started teaching children, I soon realized that I had never had to work to learn a subject. Most subjects and skills came easily to me and if I found something hard, like math, I simply avoided it. Nobody taught me to write, beyond the outlining skills we learned in fifth grade, and I had taught myself to read before I went to kindergarten. I just read and wrote, and the results were always praised. I had no experience of wrestling through the necessary sequence of steps in order to master something.

This meant that when I was supposed to teach a child how to read or do multiplication, I was at a loss. I got out of this by teaching older children who already had basic skills, and teaching with someone else who took on the math part. I could reinforce skills, but not introduce them. If I wanted to be a teacher, I would have to learn about failure.

Since then, I have learned how to be a learner myself, and I've definitely learned about failure. I have seen that it can often bring us closer to the true nature of our humanity than our constant striving to be good, right and perfect.

As a language learner myself, I've learned to relinquish the purely intellectual content that keeps me on the surface of things, and sink down into deeper layers of meaning. When words don't make sense, you have to read other cues: gesture, body language, facial expression, tone of voice. You have to try to grasp the whole, the general gist of a statement, and fill in details later. You have to admit when you don't understand, and ask for help. And you have to laugh at your mistakes, or else you'll be constantly crying.

I was always terrified to do anything like this when I was at school. I clung to correctness like a crutch. But I've finally started to learn the lesson that Brendan had tried to teach me years ago, with his first, stumbling steps: falling down is not a permanent disaster, but a temporary condition from which one can bounce up again and again. Therein lies the secret of the Resurrection, which turned the most immense failure ever into the greatest source of joy.

The Pharisees, who want to take refuge in being right, will never learn this secret. Only when we are able to release the compulsion to always be correct, to allow ourselves to make mistakes and laugh and move onward, can we relax into a greater stream of life.

That is what I now want to learn how to do, more than acquiring any technique or skill or qualification: how to relax, to let go, to take joy in the process as it unfolds, not needing to fix and determine and control everything. Only then can life, that wondrous and ever-evolving mystery, enter into me with its healing power.

> *Meditation*
>
> Is it lawful to heal on the Sabbath, or not?

16.
Ten Lepers:
Luke 17:11–19

Turned Back

For ten good men
God would have saved
a city doomed
to perish in flames.

But ten good men
could not be found.
Corruption reigned.
The city burned.
The righteous fled.

And one, unsaved,
was turned to salt,
to stand forever
looking back.

Even before
my skin turned to salt
I was one of the untouchables.

A Samaritan stands beyond the pale
for the ones who turn
toward Zion's hill,

always to be kept
at a distance, apart
from the righteous, uncorrupted ones.

And never, never allowed to return
to the heart of their life,
to the God of their truth.

Now here we stand
in the space between:
nine men who might be good enough,
and one apart,
a leper among lepers.

I can stand among them,
but am not one of them.
I can cry out with them,
but their God will not hear me.

I can look back to the life I lost
and stand like a pillar
pointing nowhere.

But here comes life
along the road.
Here he is,
the Living One,
the one who will hear me,
the one who will answer,
the one who despises
nothing that lives.

Let the life in me rise
and break through my salt.
Let the pillar be gone.
I will find a new direction.
I will point toward *him*.

Let the others go on their righteous way.
I will not move without giving thanks
to the one who turns toward our salvation.

He didn't have to look for us.
He didn't have to hear our cry.
He could have gone on, but he turned back.
He turned me back to myself.

And now
forever
I turn
to him.

Reflections on Ten Lepers

The number ten has a prominent place in Jewish lore – the Ten Commandments and the ten plagues of Egypt to name just a couple. In rabbinic Judaism, ten became the number of men required to form a quorum for worship (a minyan). The sages taught that whenever ten worshippers were gathered, the Divine Presence dwelled among them.

When considering the significance of this number in Luke's story of the healing of the ten lepers, I thought of another sort of quorum: the ten men needed in order for the corrupted cities of Sodom and Gomorrah to be saved from destruction. The Lord had heard of their depravity and was sending his angels to judge and do away with the wicked. But Abraham pleaded, 'Will you sweep away the righteous with the wicked?' Finally he reached an agreement with the Lord: if ten righteous men could be found, the cities would be spared.

The cities were so wicked, however, that the Lord decided to destroy them. Abraham's nephew Lot was permitted to flee, along with his wife and two daughters. They were warned not to look back as burning sulfur rained down on Sodom and Gomorrah, but Lot's wife couldn't help it and was turned into a pillar of salt (see Genesis, chapters 18 and 19).

Abraham's daring to argue with the Lord shows that the relationship between humans and the divine is not one of unquestioning obedience to an overwhelming authority. There is room to evolve a new way of thinking, one that cares more for the vulnerable minority than for unilateral justice, and asserts that even the wicked must remain if it means not destroying a seed of goodness in their midst. Though the cities did not escape destruction, those with a connection to the new stream of Abraham and his future blessing of all humanity were allowed to flee. But they were not all able to make it to safety. Looking back to the past sometimes impedes us on our way forward.

The healing of the ten lepers takes place just as Christ Jesus has turned on his way toward Jerusalem and the cross. The lepers call to him, 'Jesus, Master, have mercy on us.' He tells them to go and show themselves to the priests, and on their way they realize they are healed. Simply picking ourselves up and moving toward wholeness can sometimes be a healing factor in itself.

But in this story a further step is taken by the one who turns back to thank Jesus. In this case he is not turning back to the past, like Lot's wife, but turning to the future, to the one who will show all humanity the way toward healing. And this future needs to involve a change in our ideas of who is good and worthy of salvation.

The man who turns back is a Samaritan, a term that has become connected with goodness and compassion in modern minds because of Luke's own parable of the Good Samaritan. In fact, a *good* Samaritan would have been a paradox to Jews in the time of Jesus. The Samaritans were descended from the remnant of the inhabitants in the northern kingdom of Israel who had mixed with foreign peoples during the time of the Assyrian deportation in 721 BC. They were considered tainted and impure by the Jews of the southern kingdom of Judah who returned from their own Babylonian captivity to rebuild the Temple hundreds of years later, and they were not permitted to help with the reconstruction or worship there.

The Samaritans themselves, meanwhile, who only recognized the five books of Moses and rejected later additions to the Hebrew scriptures, felt themselves to be the holders of a more ancient tradition, the true keepers of the old Judaic religion. They built their own temple on Mount Gerizim and continued to worship the Lord in their own way.[1]

In the story of the Samaritan woman at the well in the Gospel of John, reference is made to those who worship 'in spirit and in truth' (John 4:23). It doesn't matter on which mountain or in which temple you worship; what matters is that you recognize the true source of healing. And that is what the Samaritan who turns back to thank Jesus does.

'Rise and go your way, your faith has made you well,' Jesus tells him. The word used for 'arise', *anistemi*, is related to the word for resurrection, *anastasis*. In John 11:25, this is the word used in the saying, 'I am the resurrection and the life.'

As we worship in spirit and in truth, we are healed of divisions arising from inessentials. The men who did not turn back were cleansed, they underwent catharsis, but were they truly healed? We need to add another step to the process, an awakening to the source of our blessings, turning toward it to form a new relationship full of love, mutual acceptance and gratitude. This does not happen unconsciously as we walk dully along our usual paths. It is an inner awakening of the true self: an activity that can be called 'faith', which leads to resurrection. In this event, the 'change of heart and mind', the *metanoia* that John the Baptist proclaimed in the wilderness that must lead to new life for humanity, is pictured.

When that turning takes place, it produces a free and spontaneous outflow of gratitude. We recognize what the divine world has done for us, how it brings us into existence and gives us sustenance and healing in every circumstance of our lives. Cultivating that sense of gratitude is itself a healing force that cleanses and strengthens us, making us whole by reuniting us with the sources of our life.

Personal Connections – Part 16

One day, I was doing laundry in our apartment building in Switzerland. My son had suddenly run out of clean clothes and I was in a hurry. When I saw a finished load sitting in the machine, I took it out and quickly shoved mine in – something I usually never do, but I had so little time before I had to go to work and it needed to be done.

A few minutes later, the doorbell rang. I opened the door and was confronted by Louise, our downstairs neighbor. She glared at me and poured out a stream of invective in French that I struggled to comprehend. Terrible – inexcusable – horrible!

What on earth had I done? Eventually I deciphered Louise's message. She had had two loads of laundry, not one, and the second one had been waiting to go into the machine when her first was done. I had vaguely seen this but thought both were finished, or rather, in my haste to get my own laundry done, I didn't really think about it at all. If I had realized, I would never have stolen her machine. But she seemed to think I had deliberately insulted her with this atrocious deed.

I felt assaulted by this sudden barrage, then angry. Why was she making such a fuss? Why did she assume malice on my part? I struggled to express myself in French, but kept forgetting simple words like 'laundry' and 'unintentional'; I sounded like an idiot. Losing my patience, I snapped that she shouldn't speak to me like that. Naturally this made things even worse.

Then there was the linguistic problem of whether I should use the more formal '*vous*' to address her or the more familiar and friendly '*tu*'. This is a gray area for adult acquaintances, and always hard for English speakers to negotiate with all the unspoken social currents it stirs up. I had never talked to Louise much myself, but my husband had. Were we on a '*tu*' basis? I decided to say '*vous*' instead, but this only seemed to enrage her even further. I had meant it as a sign of respect, but she must have taken it to mean that I was treating her like a complete stranger.

I managed to stop the invective by stomping downstairs and taking my own unfinished laundry out of the machine. Louise said I didn't have to, but I insisted. Then I closed the door on her and sat down with my wet laundry, shaken to the core, trying to calm my disturbed breathing and racing heartbeat. It was like a replay of my encounter with the landlady, back in my twenties in Seattle. I'd done something wrong. I'd offended someone, but hadn't meant to (although at least this time it was in the course of trying to be clean instead of dirty).

I felt unjustly attacked; Louise's reaction was out of all proportion to my offense. My instinct was to retreat and defend myself, reacting to her angry accusations with angry accusations of my own. I could shout back at her, if only in my head, and criticize her for her unfairness and unwillingness to listen.

Or I could remember what I learned many years ago: that admitting I'd done something wrong would not kill me. Nor did it mean that I had to lose my dignity and accede to the image of myself as a horrible person. I could correct the fault, learn from it and move on. More than that, I could try to repair the relationship that had been wounded by my wrongdoing.

After I had calmed down, I thought of a way to apologize and make amends. I bought a small lavender plant for Louise, who was a passionate gardener and kept our building looking nice with seasonal plants and decorations. I wrote a note explaining that I was sorry for removing her laundry, that I had not meant to upset her, and it wouldn't happen again. I thanked her for the beautiful decorations and said how much we appreciated them. I left this appeasing gift by Louise's door.

Focusing on what is positive, what I can sincerely praise or be grateful for, helps me when I'm caught in a storm of negative accusation. It doesn't wish away the negative, but it gives something to cultivate and grow in the midst of destruction. And I have also come to believe that no relationship should ever be thrown away or destroyed without the utmost efforts to preserve it. Relationships are our most precious possession, the fabric of our life.

Sometimes, relationships must be set aside for another time when we are stronger. But I thought I'd make an effort to repair this one. The next time I saw Louise, she smiled radiantly and poured out her thanks as effusively as she'd previously ranted about how horrible I was. My little gesture of thoughtfulness and noticing her contribution to our shared space seemed to have worked. I was invited to say *tu* and could now pass her in the hallway with a clear conscience.

This might seem like a trivial incident, but for me it represented a huge step forward. It took almost thirty years for me to learn how to value relationships and work with them in this way, how to respond to assaults on my worth as a human being without becoming 'overwhelmed, enraged, ashamed, or collapsed'.[2] This took an enormous amount of schooling, not through official, formal programs, but through the most wonderful, most challenging school there is: the school of human relationships. This is the school of love, led by our master teacher, Christ Jesus. And in this schooling my wisest, best teachers have been the ones who appear most weak and powerless: children, those with disabilities, the voiceless and vulnerable ones, the wounded ones. It was they who brought the wisdom that I needed, humbly waiting for me to approach them, to set aside my prejudices and defenses, and see with new eyes.

My early life had left me unprepared for this schooling, weakened by the dance of withdrawal and retreat in which I shied away from the areas in me that most needed my attention and care. But somewhere inside me, beneath the level of conscious awareness, another stream had been at work, pulling me back into life and community and inner integration, while outer circumstances presented me with new possibilities and the opportunity to make new choices.

Luke's story, in which a man who is doubly an outcast – both a leper and a Samaritan – is the only one to awaken to a higher level of awareness through gratitude for his healing, reminds me how important it is to cultivate my own sense of gratitude for all I have received. Not only for healing, but also for the illness that allows me to know the power of healing; not only for the homecoming, but also for the journey into distant, uncomfortable and frightening places that enables me to truly know, appreciate, and value home upon my return. Gratitude for the gift of life, and for all that enables me to live, can germinate in the place of emptiness, and when it grows and expands, it makes me strong to receive all the further gifts God wants to bestow upon me.

> *Meditation*
> Rise and go your way, your faith
> has made you well.

17.
A Blind Man of Jericho:
Mark 10:46–52

Blind Bartimaeus[1]

It's a heavy fate,
a child born blind.
Everyone wonders
what sin runs so deep
it even tainted
the seed in the womb.
Everyone turns
their eyes away,
not wanting to look
on the luckless one
and maybe be marked
by his sightlessness.

As a child, I didn't know what I lacked.
I felt the closed-in, lowering gloom
that you call 'dark', and the lifting, expanding,

opening up, the radiance of 'light'.
I felt the sun rise, when the world sang for joy,
and the chill as a shadow crossed its face.

Light streamed to me from my mother's face,
her smile, her laugh, her gentle kiss.
Darkness fell when she turned from me
with silent tears, my future her grief.

My father illumined my mind with words,
opening to me the book of our people,
the story of how God called all things
to be and become, beginning with light.
He told how that light was so often lost –
obscured in the foolish hearts of men,
exiled from Eden for doubting God's love,
losing faith in the wilderness,
blindly stumbling after false gods.

But the light will come to us again.
He will always be there, beyond the clouds,
creating, illumining, turning his face
to shine upon us,
calling us
to remember our name,
to lift up our hearts,
to ourselves become light.

My father taught me to stand upright
in spite of the weight of my destiny,

accepting my fate as a sign of trust.
So what if I couldn't live on my own,
and had to beg for my daily bread?
No man survives alone. We are all, every one,
beggars before the mercy of God,
dependent on grace, and may God help
the one who is blind to that truth.

That's what I tried to show my people
as I sat each day by the side of the road,
my bowl held open
to heaven's gifts.

But their eyes were closed.
They didn't see
the sun that had risen in their midst,
the light of the world,
the face of God.

I wouldn't have asked him for sight for myself.
I was used to the dark, and it suited me.
I could wait for the day when all things would cast off
their earthly garments, and stand in his light.

But I could see
he wanted to show them –
the ones whose hearts
were not all stone,
the ones who might yet
be brought to the light

by seeing a blind man
seeing again.

So I called to him, as he called me.
I threw off my covering and leapt into light,
following him on his way into shadow.

Let the blind man die.
Let him be reborn,
made new in a new world,
called by the Word
that created light:

Let *us* be…

Reflections on *A Blind Man of Jericho*

The healing of a blind man (or two men, according to Matthew) takes place in each of the four gospels shortly before Jesus enters Jerusalem at the beginning of Holy Week. There are many highly significant differences between the accounts, and while a more thorough, in-depth study of them is beyond the scope of this book, even a brief consideration makes it clear that this healing is of great importance.

The three Synoptic Gospels name the location of this healing as Jericho. Since they depict Jesus as making only one journey from Galilee on the way to his Crucifixion in Jerusalem, it signifies that he is nearing his goal. Jericho is depicted in the Hebrew Bible as the first city the Israelites conquered after crossing the Jordan into the Promised Land (Joshua, Chapter 6). It sits more than 800 feet (245 meters) below sea level in the Jordan plain, nearly 3,500 feet (1,065 meters) below Jerusalem, which is only 17 miles (27 kilometers) away. Located at an important crossroads on the trade routes, it was known as an oasis in the midst of the desert and called the City of Palms. It thus represents a low point in the journey, a descent preceding the great ascent to Golgotha. It also serves as a symbol of the danger posed by materialistic thinking.

Loss of physical sight is not the greatest misfortune we can face. The greatest tragedy we can imagine is the possibility that we will not develop eyes to see the spiritual reality that underlies all existence, and which will remain when our transitory sense world has passed away. If we do not use our time in the sensory world to develop this vision, then we will be helpless in future conditions of existence. We will lose our freedom and independence and be reduced to complete poverty of soul.

It is this spiritual vision, which simultaneously imparts a spiritual understanding, that Christ Jesus seeks to teach his disciples. The healings have all addressed the inner capacities of the human being, through images of cleansing, re-enlivening and repairing the physical body. Now comes a final demonstration.

In the Gospel of Mark, the blind man is called Bartimaeus, meaning 'Son of Timaeus'. It is a peculiar etymology, because 'Bar' is Hebrew and 'Timaeus' is Greek. Many theories have been proposed for this strange coupling, but in looking at the healings as a whole I made a connection with the very first in the series: the demon-possessed man in the synagogue of Capernaum. Recall that when Jesus rebukes the demon, the word usually translated as 'rebuke' is *epitimao* in Greek, and it was said that *timao* means 'to honor'. This is also the root of the name Timaeus. Thus, in the healing of Bartimaeus, the Son of Honor, we have reaped the fruits of that first healing. We are shown what is possible when we learn to suffer in the right way through all struggles that come to meet us in the physical world: our trials and obstacles, our illnesses and handicaps. It is the culmination of the path of faith and trust in the divine will that those who are healed by Christ Jesus demonstrate to us.

The motif of twoness or doubling underlies all the healings of blindness. In the earlier healing of a blind man at Bethsaida in Mark, as we have seen, it is a two-stage process. In each of the three accounts of the healing at Jericho in the Synoptic Gospels, the man calls out to Jesus twice, the second time after the crowd rebukes him and tells him to be silent. There is that word, *epitimao*, again, now representing a counter-healing impulse: the period for silent catharsis has passed; it is time to speak out.

As mentioned above, in Matthew, two blind men are healed, and the incident at Jericho is the second such healing that he describes with a very similar pattern. The first took place just after the raising of Jairus's daughter and so is connected with resurrection. This second healing is the last in Matthew before Christ's own resurrection.

In John's Gospel, the man does not call out, instead he is brought before the Pharisees for questioning twice. He also encounters Jesus twice, the second time receiving full knowledge of the being of the Son of Man. The twofold nature of seeing is also indicated in cryptic sayings that recall the ones surrounding the feeding of the multitude, and like them echo the Hebrew prophets:

> 'For judgment I came into this world that those who do not see may see, and those who see may become blind.' Some of the Pharisees near him heard these things, and said to him, 'Are we also blind?' Jesus said to them, 'If you were blind you would have no guilt; but now that you say, "We see," your guilt remains.' (John 9:39–41)

The greatest danger for the human being today is not climate change, political unrest, epidemics or anything else coming at us from outside. It is that we will lose our sense of life, that we will no longer be able to choose life over death because we cannot tell the difference between them, or we actually prefer the state of death to life. It is a crisis of perception and discernment that requires us to assess the way in which we see.

There are two kinds of seeing, one that is suited to the sense world and one to the spiritual world, and neither is better than the other. The sickness, or the 'guilt', comes in when we confuse the two, when we cannot pass from one to the other when necessary or apply them in appropriate ways. True sickness lies in not knowing one is sick, and true blindness in not knowing one is blind. That is the error of the

Pharisees, whose intellectual prowess, derived from the sense world, leads to the danger of their losing touch with the living presence of God in their midst. The 'judgment' that Christ Jesus brings should not be understood as condemnation. It is rather the healing force that can restore correct judgment in our own minds and mode of perception. It frees us from error and delusion, and brings us back into right relationship with the divine. That is the goal of all the healings, now brought to its fullest expression in the healing of Bartimaeus.

When we know our own blindness, when we understand that seeing with physical senses blinds us to the spirit, and that seeing in the spirit requires us to let go of certain habits and fixed ideas, then our guilt is lifted. We will no longer make the kind of mistakes that spring from ignorance, imperviousness, and reluctance to learn or change. We will be able to cry out for Christ's healing power, which also teaches us how to use our higher senses again.

Of the four accounts, only John specifies that the blind man was born blind, but in drawing on the Gospel of Mark for inspiration I have taken the liberty of imagining Bartimaeus as having been born blind as well. In a way we are all born blind: birth into the sense world brings with it blindness to our spiritual origins, and learning to see can never be a matter only for our physical eyes.[2]

In most translations when Jesus asks, 'What do you want me to do for you?' the man responds, 'Lord, let me recover my sight,' which suggests that he once had the power of vision. But the word used is *anablepo*, which actually means to look upward. What the man prays for is the upward-looking vision that reconnects us to our spiritual home and our divine parent. It is not a contradiction for a man born blind to ask to see again, for we all saw in the spiritual world before our birth. It is this vision that we have lost and need to recover.

When we recover our spiritual vision, the most important thing we can see is Christ himself, who is our teacher and guide in higher realms of knowledge.[3] The man in the story senses Christ's presence without physical sight, and calls out: 'Jesus, son of David, have mercy on me!' He already has a secure grasp on an inward way of seeing that releases him from a too-powerful attachment to sense impressions. He will be able to see clearly in both worlds, keeping his eyes upon Christ and seeing through all of the confusing and deceptive phenomena thrown at human beings by the adversarial forces working in the sense world.

This is something the disciples are still struggling with. As they experience the trial of the Crucifixion it is by no means certain that they will manage to maintain their vision of Christ when death robs them of his sense-perceptible presence. The healing of the blind man is a final instruction for them to look upward, and one that they must learn if they are not to be thrown back by the devastating events to come.

Personal Connections – Part 17

I thought that my migraine headaches might get better with menopause, but they didn't. They merely detached themselves from my monthly cycle and struck unpredictably, generally waking me around 4.00 am and lasting until late into the afternoon. I started to have them more frequently, two or three times a month. Besides struggling with the change to my diet and investigating what else might help me with my other symptoms, I would from time to time be confined to my bed for a day, in darkness, unable to move or do anything. It wasn't so much the pain in my head that was the problem as the nausea. The slightest bit of light or movement could cause me to retch again and again, even if there was nothing in my stomach. I was unable to hold down even a sip of water.

As I lay there in the dark, eyes covered with a damp washcloth, I wondered, 'What am I not seeing?' In the constant rush to get things done in everyday life, was I missing something? Was I overlooking something that was causing my body to send me this message: stop the rush, be still and quiet, look inward? There must still be something that I couldn't or didn't want to face: some barrier between my conscious awareness and darker, more unconscious phenomena.

Then, one morning, I had an emotional upset with my husband. We were talking in bed before getting up, and I said something about needing to make sure our son had everything he needed for a camping trip he was about to go on. Michael said that I babied him too much and that at fourteen he should be responsible for himself. When I got upset about this, he said he was worried about me. He was just now starting to realize how much my physical condition was weighing on me.

The remark made me angry. I couldn't believe how blind and insensitive he was not to realize that I had been unwell for a long time, and that my condition had *always* weighed me down. I also blamed him for my inability to communicate what I had been feeling: I had been too scared of him to show my real self. He wasn't bothered about my problems, he just wanted to go off and have fun with his friends. (He had in fact been out with a couple of colleagues the night before.)

I jumped out of bed and paced around, breathing hard as angry thoughts churned in my head. I tried to practice the mindfulness technique of welcoming and sitting with my feelings, but it was hard. In the end I felt compelled to express them out loud to Michael, even though I knew this was old stuff that I would regret bringing up later. He held me in his arms and listened, but didn't respond to my angry accusations. There was nothing to say, since my anger had no grounding in reality.

We left it at that and got up to begin our day, but later on, while I was helping in the weavery in the community where Michael and I both worked, these same feelings rose up again.

He doesn't care. He doesn't see me. It's so unfair.

These feelings were accompanied by a pain that struck suddenly in my abdomen and shot up into my right shoulder. I suspected that this was a gallbladder attack. I'd had several over the years, although at first I'd thought the pain was just indigestion after a heavy meal. As always, my instinct was not to tell anyone that anything was wrong with me, as if hiding the pain would make it somehow not real, and I could keep myself from being sick by not admitting it even to myself. That same instinct took over now. I left the weavery on some invented errand and went to the bathroom. I lay down on the cold tile floor and panted.

The pain didn't get better. I couldn't work like this.

At last I went back to my colleague and told her I was sick. She got me a mattress to lie down on while she called Michael to come and get me. I lay there in the hallway, feeling terrible, the angry feelings still coursing through me along with the pain. Another colleague, who was a nurse, came to check on me. The moment she touched my hand to take my pulse, I started to feel better.

Someone sees me, I thought. *Someone is taking care of me.*

The pains gradually subsided. Michael arrived and took me to the hospital to make sure it wasn't a heart attack. As I lay on a hospital bed and waited for tests and results, I contemplated my physical–emotional outburst.

In holistic medicine, as well as in the English language, the bile that is concentrated and stored in the gallbladder is associated with stored-up anger. Corrosive bile is a bodily image of rage, of the fiery feelings that can, according to their higher purpose, help us to break out of situations in which we feel helpless.

If the bile doesn't move through the system, however, if it becomes sluggish and overly thick, then it forms 'stones' of hardened cholesterol. The gallbladder can then no longer do its job of storing and releasing fluid. It, too, can become hardened and inflexible, damaged by the years of incomplete release.

My anger had gone unspoken for too long. It had been backing up and stagnating for many years. It was no wonder that I had a physical problem that was a perfect picture of this dysfunctional process.

Did the emotional dysfunction come first and affect my body, or did I have a physical weakness or imbalance that prompted a parallel emotional response?

I don't know. It could have been either, or both.

What I am sure of is that they are connected. The inner storm of raging emotions and irrational thoughts that I had experienced that morning, that I'd been unable to process and release fully, was mirrored in a painful dysfunction in my body. It was like a word with the same meaning, but spoken in two different languages.

The instinct to hide and keep it all a secret was wrapped up in this too. But I had begun to overcome that: I was no longer keeping the secret from myself, and I had started to admit that I needed help as well. I had felt a palpable relief just from the simple touch of a helping hand. That had made a profound impression on me.

I would also need to make sacrifices: my arrogant drive to manage and control everything on my own; my illusion of being wholly self-contained, which I mistook for independence; my reluctance to admit failure. My terror, really, that failure would mean exile and death.

I would have to let go of an organ that had borne all of this for so long. It had taken me too long to understand its silent word, and the pain was finally too much for it to bear. At least I could try to make sure the sacrifice would not be in vain.

My attack happened on June 24, St John's Day, exactly three years after I'd done my ritual of casting Michael's darkness from me in the form of a clay-wrapped stone dropped into a stream. Now, it seemed that I had to cast out some darkness of my own. Could that help me enter the waters of life?

I scheduled the gallbladder surgery and went into the hospital with all of this behind me. I decided to make the surgery into a sacrament, if I could. I would release something that had become sick and dysfunctional, while offering up all that I could muster as the best fruits of my soul and my life. I would make this bodily offering as a symbol of finally separating from what in me was no longer salvageable. At the same time I would strengthen my resolution to make a new relationship to the eternal truth I knew lay behind all transitory things.

The story of the blind man at Jericho speaks to me of how the night of the senses enables us to see the light of the world that shines in our deepest darkness. Perceiving this light depends upon our ability to keep our hearts open and vulnerable, even as we are assailed by the greatest griefs and deprivations. As Helen Keller, the deaf and blind writer and activist, said: 'The keenness of our vision depends not on how much we can see, but on how much we can feel.'[4] By not allowing myself to feel sorrow, I was cutting myself off from the consoling light that comes to us only when we have the courage to admit we are in the dark.

My body, fortunately, was wiser and refused to be quiet. In the face of all I had done to suppress it, it had finally shouted out like the blind man who keeps on calling to Jesus.

As the anaesthetic took hold and darkness descended, I vowed never again to make myself so blind, so impervious, so insensitive to the messages of my body, which came from a hidden wisdom deep inside me. I didn't know quite how I would navigate the next steps toward finding out what it was that my true self really wanted. I only knew the old world had to come to an end.

> *Meditation*
>
> What do you want me to do for you?

18.

Lazarus:

John 11:1–44

What the Rich Young Man Said

He told me to sell everything,
give all to the poor, and follow him.
Yes, I turned away – but don't harshly judge
the one who won't let go.

It's not that I can't give up the things
I love to see and touch:
this silver cup I've had from childhood,
that tapestry of woven silk –
a gift from my dear mother –
or luxuries like roasted meat,
soft pillows, scented baths.
I could renounce all these and eat
the crusts thrown to the beggars
if it brought me endless life.
I'd call that a good bargain.

But what of all the other lives
that rest on mine, so interlaced
I can't say where I end and they begin?
My loyal serving maids and men,
the tenant farmers who depend
on me as their kind master?
My sisters, too, who look to me
for guidance and support –
if I abandon them, what care
and understanding will they find
in this harsh world? I can't
just leave them to pursue
a selfish dream of life.

I'd also miss how they care for me,
their voices, their laughter, their hands in mine,
the way we rejoice and mourn together,
our silent communion in which I can rest,
knowing myself to be known by them.

These human bonds are my treasure,
these relations are my wealth.
Without them I'll be more than poor,
I'll lose myself. For what am I
apart from all that links me to life?
Who am I, if not their kind master,
beloved brother, devoted friend?
If I lose these ties, what will be left?
Won't I die, in truth, if I give up all this
and bind myself only to him?

And yet, that's what he told me,
and I must listen, or be dead indeed.

At death, it's true, all human ties
are broken, and we walk alone
into that unknown country
with nothing, no one.
No, not one.

By binding loved ones to myself,
valuing them as possessions, things,
objects to control and manage,
I'm killing something singular
in them, and in myself.
Yes, even caring bonds must break
if we are to know freedom.

Their value is not only for me.
I must set them free to value themselves,
to make their own ways, as I make mine,
and trust that our ways
will lead us all home
on the day of celebration.

So I will die before I die.
I will go into that dark cave
of my own separate body
to walk alone where no one else,
not even he, can enter.

And when my limbs grow cold and numb,
no movement left, flesh limp as rags,
I will trust his way of loneliness
to lead me toward a greater love
than dead minds can conceive:
a family unbound by race or blood,
a kingdom where power does not rule,
a priesthood of all who offer their hearts –
our human future reborn.

I will lose the mind
that knows only old things.
I will become new.
I will hear his call
with the whole of myself
and answer him
with my body, my soul,
my life given up
to the way of his Word –

Lazarus,
come forth!

Reflections on Lazarus

In the Gospel of John one last healing takes place before the entry into Jerusalem: the raising of Lazarus. This is not a healing in the same category as most of the others, but rather a mystery drama of initiation. However, because all the healing stories represent stages along the way to a new form of initiation, one intended for all humanity, Lazarus must be considered as a final step in that process.

This initiation is obliquely referred to in the other three Gospels with the story of a wealthy young man or ruler who asks Jesus for the secret of eternal life. This takes place after Jesus has crossed into Judea, shortly before his third and final foretelling of his death and resurrection. According to early apocryphal sources, the rich young man is identified with the Lazarus who was raised after three days in the tomb.[1]

In Mark, this identity is hinted at with the words: 'Jesus, looking at him, loved him' (Mark 10:21). Likewise, 'Jesus loved Martha and her sister and Lazarus' (John 11:5). Such love does not only express a personal emotion, but the bond between initiate and student. Unlike in English, in Greek there are several words for 'love'. The word used in both of these verses is *agapao*, which is not familial love or friendship or erotic love. It can be defined as a love that cares for and esteems the beloved according to their own nature and needs, with no regard for the benefit or pleasure of the lover. Thus God loves the Son, and the Son loves those who are able to rise from death through the new mysteries that he is about to establish with his deed on Golgotha.[2]

The older form of initiation involved the presence of the hierophant and a circle of other spiritual masters who guided the initiand through a dangerous process. If these masters were not present and in control at every step, there were severe risks involved in loosening oneself from the security of the physical body and seeking to enter the spiritual world. The story of the young man of Nain pointed toward these dangers. It showed how Christ was able to meet a soul that had been struck down by deathly forces, encountered without sufficient preparation, and bring him back (see Chapter 7).

In the case of Lazarus, it is very puzzling that Jesus receives the news of his illness and does not go immediately to help him. His sisters must have expected that Jesus would be there to care for his student through the deathlike sleep of initiation, and they are troubled by his absence. But Christ Jesus leaves Lazarus to go through that trial alone. This is the essence of the new mysteries, which represent a new step toward freedom for the human being. The old mysteries cannot continue; they have lost their effectiveness and will even turn to evil unless the new impulse of ego-independence can come into them. Human beings must awaken not only through a process governed by the higher creative forces of life, but by means of their own inner activity that raises them up from within. For this to happen, the creative forces have to take a step back.

We speak often about human beings having faith or trust in God, but God has faith in us, too. God trusts that we are able to develop a relationship with the divine world, that we will make the transition from sensory existence to spiritual life and fulfil our highest potential as co-creators, instead of becoming slaves to destructive forces. If we do not achieve this, then a part of God's own substance will become enslaved and prey to death, for our individual ego is a gift of the divine being. We cannot be forced to awaken to this gift and respond to it with a creative gesture of our own. Only by a sort of miracle does it happen.

Jesus is affected in a profound way during this episode. He asks, 'Where have you laid him?' and 'weeps' when told to 'come and see'.

'Come and you will see' was what he said to the first disciples, when they asked him where he was staying (John 1:39). Now he is coming to see where the new human being, the Christ-bearer, is perhaps to be born. As he comes to the tomb, we are told he is 'deeply moved'. The Greek word used here, *embrimaomai*, expresses great agitation. Something previously unimaginable is about to happen: the human I has an opportunity to awaken itself from within. But this is not a given. It is a real question whether the great deed will be accomplished. Christ Jesus cannot control this; he can only call to his student, and wait.

In Christ Jesus, a high spiritual being came to earth and sacrificed his own greatness so that human beings could become great in recognizing him as the head of their communal body. But there was a risk that this would not happen, that no human would rise to the challenge. Before the Crucifixion it was necessary that at least one human being, in total freedom, took the step to become the first initiate of the new mysteries. The other disciples were not up to this level; only Lazarus could accomplish it.

We are not accustomed to thinking that God asks or even needs us to do something. Often the emphasis in Christianity is on our dependent state and how much we need the gifts of the divine world. Gratitude for those gifts and acknowledgment of our essential poverty form a crucial first step upon the path toward our higher becoming. A self-satisfied ego, pleased with its own wealth and accomplishments, cannot make the further step toward divine communion. Yet God does not want us to remain poor and dependent, but to recognize that a certain kind of loss is the only way to gain everything that matters.

In considering the story of the rich young man, it seemed to me that he could not have been motivated by greed and selfish materialism to hang on to his possessions. He was clearly a highly developed soul, worthy of the love of Christ Jesus. His reluctance to let go of his wealth must refer to another kind of possessiveness, perhaps to the difficulty we experience when we are called to become our true selves. The path toward the higher ego is a lonely one, and we must disconnect from everything and everyone around us before we can return to life and community.

Relationships often involve unconscious ties through which we tug and pull on each other, keeping one another in bondage without being aware of what we are doing. To let go of those bonds so that others can be free involves a terrifying moment of total isolation, truly a death experience.

Lazarus, the young man so rich in capacities of soul and spiritual wisdom, was able to accomplish this because of his faithful love, his trust in Christ Jesus. He knew that although he must endure a time of aloneness and apparent death, his Teacher would call to him and show him the way out.

That call is difficult to translate accurately. It is usually rendered as 'Come forth!', but in Greek there is no verb, no word of command. Instead, it means something like 'Lazarus, out to here'.[3]

When, through earlier stages of healing, we are able to hear the voice of Christ, it tells us which way to go. He is always there for us, but it is up to us to move ourselves. If we can turn toward him, even in the midst of an oppressive, frightening, tomb-like dark night of the soul, the promise of mutual trust between God and humanity is fulfilled.

Personal Connections – Part 18

The year after my surgery, Brendan was in the ninth grade at a Rudolf Steiner school near us in Switzerland. In two and a half years he'd had to adapt to a new culture, new classmates, and several new languages.

He'd done amazingly well. He had mastered Swiss German and been integrated into the social life of the class, but he still faced some challenges. He'd always been distracted in school. Some of his former teachers found him very frustrating, and sometimes said he was being lazy. This gave Brendan the impression that he was dumb and incapable. There had been a suggestion that he had ADHD and should get tested. I wasn't averse to that, although I was definitely opposed to giving him drugs or any other harsh interventions, but our life fell into chaos and we moved before anything could be done about it.

The topic came up again when Brendan suddenly took it into his head that he wanted to do the admissions test for the Gymnasium, the type of school that tracked for college entrance in the Swiss system. Michael and I didn't say no, because we didn't want to oppose any kind of initiative he took to learn something. Brendan was usually uninterested and unmotivated when it came to study. Maybe he was finally going to push himself to pay attention and get somewhere, I thought.

But his teacher was concerned. There was no way Brendan could handle such an intense academic program right now, she told us. The very idea was distracting him from the work he was supposed to be doing in school, where he remained extremely unfocused and was not completing his tasks properly. She did not recommend he take the test.

I wanted to tell her that we were not pushing Brendan academically; we appreciated who he was and just wanted to encourage him in whatever he chose to do. I also thought she should know something about Brendan's background, about his developmental delay in his first months and about the depression that had marred my early bonding with him.

We arranged to meet and we had a good conversation. I felt that this teacher really heard me and understood something important about Brendan. However, something disturbing also came up during our talk. Brendan had just started a two-week work placement, where the students were supposed to try out a profession of interest to them. Brendan had procrastinated until the last minute, then, pushed slightly by me, applied to a few different places related to gardening, architecture and cooking. All of them, at this late date, told him there was no place available. So he settled for working at a farm down the road where he had done some work already in the holidays. I didn't understand why his teacher had not done more to make sure he was getting a placement early enough.

His teacher told us a different story, however. She said that Brendan had told her weeks ago that he was going to work at this farm, and she'd been glad to hear it. She thought he looked tired and a little peaked, and the farm work was just what he needed. During a forestry block at the beginning of the year Brendan had worked calmly and tirelessly on physical projects that the other students found boring or burdensome. He had been dependable, thorough, and highly thought of by the supervising foresters. It brought out a totally different side to him than the scattered, spaced-out boy she usually saw in school.

I was not surprised that he did better in the forest than the classroom; he'd always been an outdoor-oriented boy. What disturbed me was that he had told two totally different stories, created two separate worlds to inhabit. If he'd already told his teacher he was going to work at the farm, why tell us he had to find a place? Was he developing a mental 'split' similar to my own, in which he repressed content that he thought would be unacceptable for one audience or another? Was he, like me, in hiding from himself?

I'd learned from current brain research that his ADHD-like behavior could be at least partly caused by trauma, and the distance that had grown up between him and me, I had also learned, was a source of trauma for a small child. The withdrawal of a parent, particularly the mother as the usual primary caregiver, causes an existential crisis for a child because it is a threat to their very survival. This applies not only to physical loss or absence, but to inner or emotional withdrawal. Emotional bonding is as necessary as physical food and shelter. Without it, a child cannot thrive, and may internalize a state of anxiety that affects the brain and disrupts learning. Many children labelled as having an 'attention deficit' are displaying hypervigilant behavior. This causes them to constantly monitor their environment for any threats and react to stimuli that others don't even notice. The remedy is to apply calming, reassuring, regulating processes that defuse such vigilance and allow for higher-level learning to take place.[4]

Brendan's sudden wish to go to another school, I felt, was a kind of threat response – a reaction to fears that he was dumb and inadequate, and which led him to want to escape his circumstances. Running away from his problems, however, would not help. I agreed with the teacher that he should give up the idea of going to Gymnasium and that we would talk to him about it. I also shared my concern about the two stories he had told. We would need to keep an eye on this and see what we could do to support him.

The next day, she asked if we would be willing to attend a faculty meeting where I could share what I had told her about Brendan's early years, and about my depression and its traumatic effects. The teachers could then more consciously hold Brendan in their awareness and meditatively carry him, creating a new possibility for change. This sort of 'Child Study' was done in Waldorf schools for students who were having difficulty, and it frequently had a strong effect.

I said that this would be wonderful and we set a date for the meeting. On that day I had a migraine headache, but I was determined to go. I vomited in the bushes following our half-hour car ride down the mountain, but I managed to hold myself together for the next hour.

It was still in the days of COVID and we sat in a large, widely spaced circle in the school hall, a group of about twenty-five people. I described Brendan's birth, the feeding problems that made his early days so difficult, and my bleak mental and emotional state. I knew now I'd suffered from postpartum depression, but at the time I felt it was just my own inexpressible badness and was too ashamed to reveal it to anyone. I mentioned the lag in Brendan's motor development which seemed to go away when he learned to walk but was maybe still hidden somehow in his brain.

I said that what concerned me most was that Brendan had gotten the idea that he was dumb and lazy, and that he was trying to escape from himself. Michael and I accepted who he was and just wanted to give him the best chance to express his own wonderful gifts. I hoped that the teachers would support us in that.

As I thought back to those days of depression, I knew that back then I could never have imagined that I would someday be telling my terrible secret to a large group of people. Now, I did not care one bit whether Brendan's teachers judged or criticized me. I didn't think they would, but in any case that was not what mattered. What mattered was our beautiful child and his future. I didn't care what I had to give up, what it might cost me in terms of pride or material goods or anything else. I only wanted to remove as many of the obstacles in his way as I could, and set him free to become himself. I was sorry for the obstacles I had put there myself. But if this meeting could help to remove any of them, I was glad.

A week later Brendan's teacher told us that she'd seen a big change in his ability to focus. It was as if a weight really had been lifted off him.

In the early days of his life, he hadn't been real to me yet. He'd still been too much a part of myself, reminding me of things that I didn't want to acknowledge or support – a weak, needy part that I strove to ignore and deny. He'd persisted, though, until he became real to me as his own undeniably separate self, whom I learned to love and honor for his own sake.

Through knowing Brendan, I became more secure in myself. I gained a grip on a corner of reality. My attitude toward my own weakness changed, as I saw that human beings need to become vulnerable in order to grow. That has been the fruit of my own journey as a mother, and the gift of our child's presence in our lives. I want so much to give that gift back to him, so that he can fully take hold of his own reality.

This does not mean that I have an unhealthy impulse to suffocate my own potential, or to live out my own unlived dreams through my child. It only means that I know we are all a part of a great dance in which we each take turns to step into the spotlight for a while before stepping back to the sidelines to watch. And all of us are carried and embraced by our love and interest and appreciation for each other, woven together in a fabric of joyful creative purpose that lifts us all to a higher level.

Adolescence is a time when both child and parent go through the trials of death and rebirth. How can one give birth to a new adult, ready to navigate a challenging world on his own, without either over-protecting or abandoning him? It is a test that shows whether the previous years of preparation have produced the necessary transformation in our hearts.

In the initiation drama he enacts with Lazarus, Christ shows us a way. Inwardly groaning, as with the labor pains of a mother, he lets his pupil cross over a threshold alone to experience the full weight of his earthbound tomb and the separateness of an isolated ego. He waits for this to happen, but then comes close again and stands at the door. He does not exert his divine authority to command an awakening. He merely indicates that he is there, and invites his beloved to join him in the wider world where a new life can begin. He takes a step back so that a new being can be stirred to movement, taking his place in the sacred dance.

Through the life experiences he brought to me, Christ challenged me to give birth to a new being within myself: a lover, a mother, a child, both vulnerable and strong. Learning how to dance has been painful and frustrating and full of failure, but I may be finally getting the hang of it. If I fall, I'll just laugh and get up again. No death can keep me down forever when I learn to have trust in the resurrecting power of love.

> ### *Meditation*
> I am the resurrection and the life.

Afterword

It's been about a year and a half since that meeting. Brendan is finishing tenth grade and taking up his tasks with grace and determination. He is growing calmer and more focused than before, although school remains a challenge. He'll stay a few more years in the Steiner school while he decides his next steps. Whatever profession he chooses, I know that he will be a light for the world, as he has been for me.

I can never give him back the lost years when I was not able to be really present for him, with all my unpenetrated darkness. But I can strive to be there for him now, to hold him emotionally, as teenagers desperately need us adults to do, however they may appear to push us away. I can cultivate the eyes and ears that perceive his unfolding reality, and express my enduring delight in the mere fact of his being. And I believe that this can help to mitigate, if not to undo, the mistakes of my past.

My proudest moment as a parent came when Brendan said he was glad he could talk to me about his feelings. I can't ask for anything more than that, and it gives me hope for his future. At least if he is able to communicate, he can never be trapped in the prison of silent shame as I was. As Bessel van der Kolk says, 'Communicating fully is the opposite of being traumatized.'[1]

I am sad that I was never able to communicate fully with my eurythmy teachers, but as the years pass and the pain subsides, I am filled with gratitude for all I received through the eurythmy training. I learned so much during those years I spent swimming, and sometimes drowning, in the substance of love, not least through my failures. I wish I could share what I learned with my teachers, as I was unable to do at the time. With this book, at least, I have been able to articulate much that I could not express then, and maybe that will be a step toward opening the conversation again.

I've continued to learn about my outstanding symptoms and health issues. My headaches didn't stop after my gallbladder was removed, but I soon noticed that my emotional upsets were much less powerful. I was no longer flooded with irrational anger to the same extent, even when I felt anxious or threatened. I tried to support this positive development by strengthening my inner meditative practice, shoring up a space of calm and stillness. Thus what seemed a loss can be turned into a gift.

But I still wanted to do something about the headaches. Being blind and immobile for several days a month made it hard for me to take my own place in life. To the many therapeutic methods I'd already tried, I added more: cranio-sacral therapy, neurofeedback, probiotics, functional medicine, food elimination plans, coffee enemas, vagus nerve stimulation. But I seemed to be chasing a moving target. Every time I thought I was better, often after a sort of euphoric 'high', a headache would strike again and put me back in my bed, wondering what I was not seeing. I felt like the bleeding woman who had 'suffered much under many physicians, and had spent all that she had, and was no better but rather grew worse' (Mark 5:26).

It was discouraging, but at last I decided that I had to give up the goal of eliminating headaches. My new goal was simply to stay with myself and experience whatever was happening inside me. I might never get rid of the pain and nausea, but I could stop indulging my habit of fleeing from myself and 'things as they are'. Even the longing to be healed could become a temptation if I didn't remain firmly grounded in reality.

I began to notice a pattern of behavior whenever I suppressed my feelings, especially feelings of being criticized or judged. When those were triggered, even in a trivial way (for example, by my husband making some negative remark about the way I drive), I would either ignore them or rationalize them away, but that would often be followed by food cravings and eating urges, and a day or two later by a headache. I seemed to be living in a state of constant, low-grade anxiety, always fearful that I would be found unworthy of love and belonging. When that anxiety flared up in response to some trigger, it set off a cycle that ended with me in a state of self-protective withdrawal.

But why was I so afraid? The things that set me off were not really going to get me shunned and exiled.

I read many books about trauma and brain development, and learned how unconscious forces warp our minds and relationships. One particular book, *It Didn't Start with You* by Mark Wolynn, opened my eyes to the existence of generational trauma and epigenetics. It explained how later generations can be affected by the experiences of their ancestors, even if they are never told about them. In fact, not knowing one's family history may cause more problems than if those painful events are able to be brought to awareness and processed. Was this a clue to what had affected me?

I investigated my family history and discovered a legacy of alcoholism, mental illness, estrangement, and tragic death that I'd never fully grasped. My parents had striven to protect us from all those things. They wanted to leave that past behind, to create a different, more wholesome kind of family life – and they did. But they didn't realize that what is buried does not disappear, rather it surfaces in many mysterious ways that only make sense when one can see the whole picture. Since I was not able to cognize what I was experiencing, I only dimly felt that something was wrong, assumed it was something wrong with me, and sought relief by distancing myself from painful emotions and relationships.

According to Wolynn, when we distance ourselves from our parents, from the inheritance encoded in our bodies, it cuts off the life force that also streams to us through them. Like it or not, they are the way we entered this world, and we can't be fully in the world if we are unable to embrace that point of entry. It doesn't mean staying locked in unfree or combative relationships, but it does mean viewing our forebears with respect and compassion for their wounds, which are also our own.

As I made these connections, and learned new ways of processing experiences and feelings without shutting them down, a deeper meaning began to shine through the pain, even if my headaches didn't immediately lose their force. When I know that 'it didn't start with me' and that I am only part of a much bigger network of beings and relationships, I can work through my feelings of shame, anger and depression whenever they may arise, while still remaining engaged with my loved ones, and forgiving myself for my mistakes. I can reassure my body that my survival is not threatened by dangers now left behind in the past, and practice self-care in ways that make me more available to care for others. I can change how I relate to other people and to the world in order to meet them with a whole heart and not one fragmented by buried trauma. Instead of walling myself off with blame and judgment, I have compassion for the wounded, vulnerable human souls caught in vicious cycles of hurt and dysfunction, who need wise, loving guidance to turn them around. This, I have come to believe, is the true meaning of *metanoia* – the freely willed turning of our hearts and minds toward the good, out of trust rather than compulsion.

The truth is that human beings have a fundamental need for love and belonging, and an increasing body of evidence shows that only when this need is acknowledged and supported can deep healing take place. When we dare to make ourselves vulnerable, opening ourselves to love no matter how often we have been wounded, something truly revolutionary happens. One might even call it a miracle.

Love called to me when I was in a place of death and brought me out of my own blindness, the self-defensive structure that had become a prison. Love is also calling to you, and to every human being. May your ears and eyes be opened to the presence of the Beloved, that we all may enter into the kingdom, and join the sacred dance.

Appendix 1:
The Anthroposophical View of Christ and Human Evolution

As Rudolf Steiner often pointed out, humanity stands only at the beginning of understanding the Christ impulse and unfolding its meaning in our lives. In numerous lectures and books, Steiner sought to illuminate many riddles that otherwise remain insoluble to a modern mind. He made it possible for human beings today to set out on the path of comprehending the Christ mystery, something that will occupy us for thousands of years to come.

For me, such elucidation was essential. Although I was attracted to Christianity, there were just too many holes and disjunctions in what I had received from tradition for me to fully enter into it. Not everyone may need this kind of understanding, but it plays an important role in my personal experience and thus in the reflections contained in this book. For those unfamiliar with the anthroposophical view of Christ and of human evolution, I offer this brief outline as an orientation. If there are any startling or unfamiliar elements, I hope that readers will give them a fair hearing and approach them with an open mind. Testing new thoughts against one's experiences and discerning whether they lead to fruitful paths of further inquiry is how we can feel our way toward truth and not remain locked in our prejudices and old ways of thinking.

There have been many ways of understanding the nature and relationship of Jesus and Christ throughout the centuries. Rudolf Steiner describes Jesus of Nazareth as a specially prepared human being who, at the baptism in the Jordan, gave up his own human individuality or I to receive a high cosmic being from the spiritual realm of the Sun, known as the Christ-being. The creed of the Christian Community contains the statement:

> In Jesus, the Christ entered as man into the earthly world.
> The birth of Jesus upon earth is a working of the holy Spirit
> who, to heal spiritually the sickness of sin within the bodily
> nature of mankind, prepared the son of Mary to be the
> vehicle of the Christ.

The baptism in the Jordan can be considered the point of conception for Christ in the bodily sheaths of Jesus, and the following three years a time of gestation during which the Christ being had to increasingly adapt and concentrate his forces into his human vehicle. Emil Bock's book *The Three Years* explains this in detail, and is highly recommended as an overview. In turn, the Crucifixion should in a sense be considered the birth of Christ into the earthly sphere. From the Resurrection, Christ has continued to live and work in the earth, having completely transformed his earthly vessel.

A point of frequent confusion is what the Second Coming or return of Christ means. Rudolf Steiner was emphatic that Christ will not come again in a physical body, but for those with the capacity to see him, he is increasingly becoming apparent in our own time on a higher spiritual plane. It may be in fact not so much a matter of

Christ 'coming again', but rather of humanity developing new senses through which we can perceive him and work with him in a new way.[1] The sequence of healings in the gospels, I would argue, in many ways points us toward this future goal, which is already a possibility for us today.

As for his physical incarnation, why did Christ have to come at just that point in history?

This is one of those questions that was never answered satisfactorily for me by conventional Christianity. The reason becomes clearer when human history is described as a process of evolving consciousness. In the distant past, when the spiritual germ of the human being was created, we lived in communion with the spiritual world but had no independent self-consciousness. The course of human evolution has meant growing away from that spiritual consciousness into an object consciousness, where we perceive the world of nature without direct awareness of the spiritual forces behind it. This awareness has to be won again through the gateway of thinking, the spiritual activity in us that completes and integrates fragmented sense-perception, granting us access to wholeness again.

The Fall had to do with other spiritual beings who, for reasons of their own, pushed human beings too deeply into the sense world. As human beings we became cut off from our higher nature and lost touch with our origins, falling prey to a false and distorted thinking that kept us subject to the adversarial powers. Paradoxically, however, this became the opportunity for us to develop freedom. Only those who are fully divorced from the spirit can reconnect to it as the result of a free deed. In so doing they are able to integrate the newly independent human I, which can then become a gateway to the true self.

By the time of Christ's incarnation – the point of furthest descent on this journey – human beings had grown a long way toward this individual independence (the potential birth of the I), but we had also become so blind and overwhelmed by the adversarial forces that there was a real danger we would not have the strength to turn ourselves around and recover our spiritual nature. The birth of the I would then be a miscarriage.

The Christ-being, who had lovingly accompanied humanity throughout the whole course of our evolution, came at last into the long-prepared and anticipated human body of Jesus of Nazareth in order to bring his guidance and help into the physical world itself. Thus Christ united himself with earth evolution to be present for all human beings on our further course of development. This required going through the earthly death that human beings suffer, something no purely spiritual being could know or understand.

Strange though it may seem in our troubled age, with this event the point of greatest danger has been passed. The Incarnation and Resurrection of Christ brought to the earth what we need in order to overcome all that threatens us, all the challenges and dangers that face us on our way. But Christ will not counter the overpowering adversarial forces by overpowering us in their place, not even for our own good. He waits for us to turn to him and to invite him into our lives. He has made himself the servant of the goal of human evolution, in which we are to become a new order of beings who are able to love God and each other in freedom.

But for this goal to be achieved we have to wake up, to stop being deceived by the false light that entices us from two directions: over-involvement in the material world on one hand, which tempts us to deny spiritual consciousness altogether, and on the other the impulse to flee from the hardships of material existence into a delusive, self-absorbed realm of soul that is not grounded in objective spiritual reality. We have to walk between these two temptations, and Christ leads us on that path.

In our time of outward chaos and darkness, the hidden, inner light of Christ's being is becoming apparent to hearts that are open to receive him. As the Children's Service of the Christian Community puts it, again with profound simplicity: 'Christ died. He became alive in the being of those who gave him a dwelling in their hearts.' If 'God is dead' in our intellectual age, it is we who are the killers. But there is hope that resurrection can happen, through those who dare to enter the vulnerable state in which we recover our humanity through beholding the archetype of our true nature.

Not everyone uses the same earthly language to describe this, but whenever people encounter a being of Love, or a greater Self that unites them with others, or a spirit of Humanity beyond all the differences that divide us, they have an intuitive sense of Christ's activity. They can know the peace and joy that comes through connecting with the servant-leader of our earth's evolution. In this connection lies our healing, our recovery of the strength and nobility that are our birthright. In cooperation with Christ, we can turn our wills to deeds of peace and reconciliation, rather than toward destruction, enmity and strife.

Appendix 2:
The Healing Stories in the Synoptic Gospels

The following table shows the sequence of healing stories described in the Synoptic Gospels of Matthew, Mark and Luke, along with other significant events that they also share to one degree or another. The Gospel of John is very different in both structure and content, and includes only three stories that bear some relationship to the healings in the other gospels: the healing of an official's son (a centurion's servant), the healing of an invalid at the Pool of Bethesda (a paralyzed man), and the healing of a man born blind. It is the only gospel that contains an account of the Raising of Lazarus, although ancient apocryphal tradition connects the figure of Lazarus with that of the rich young man mentioned in Matthew, Mark and Luke.

MATTHEW	MARK	LUKE
Sermon on the Mount	A man with an unclean spirit	A man with an unclean spirit
A leper	A woman with a fever	A woman with a fever
A centurion's servant	A leper	A leper
A woman with a fever	A paralyzed man	A paralyzed man
——	A man with a withered hand	A man with a withered hand
——	——	A centurion's servant
——	——	The Young Man of Nain
Jesus calms the sea		
Two demon-possessed men in the tombs	A demon-possessed man in the tombs	A demon-possessed man in the tombs
A paralyzed man	——	——
A bleeding woman and a dying girl	A bleeding woman and a dying girl	A bleeding woman and a dying girl
Two blind men	——	——
A demon-possessed man with a speech impediment	——	——
The Twelve are sent out		
A man with a withered hand	——	——
A demon-possessed blind man with a speech impediment	——	——
The Feeding of the Five Thousand		

MATTHEW	MARK	LUKE
Jesus walks on water	*Jesus walks on water*	—
A Gentile woman's daughter	A Gentile woman's daughter	
—	A deaf man with a speech impediment	—
The Feeding of the Four Thousand	*The Feeding of the Four Thousand*	—
—	A blind man	—
The Transfiguration	*The Transfiguration*	*The Transfiguration*
A boy with seizures	A boy with seizures	A boy with seizures
—	—	*The seventy are sent out*
—	—	A man with a speech impediment
—	—	A woman with a disabling spirit
—	—	A man with dropsy
—	—	Ten lepers
The rich young man	*The rich young man*	*The rich young man*
Two blind men	Blind Bartimaeus	A blind man

Notes

Preface
1. Jacques Lusseyran, *And There Was Light*, p. 239.

Introduction
1. Richard Rohr, *Falling Upward*, p. xiii.
2. See Matt. 3:1–2, Mark 1:4 and Luke 3:3.
3. To learn more about *Lectio Divina* and contemplative prayer, I recommend the work of Contemplative Outreach (contemplativeoutreach.org).

1. A Man with an Unclean Spirit: Mark 1:21–28
(See also Matthew 7:3–5 and Luke 4:31–37)
1. The Greek words used in this book are the root forms of the words, not the conjugated or declined ones used in the actual gospel text.
2. See for example Bruce D. Perry and Maia Szalavitz, *The Boy Who Was Raised as a Dog: And Other Stories From a Child Psychiatrist's Notebook*, Basic Books, USA 2017.
3. Georg Kühlewind describes the healings of 'demon-possessed' individuals as psychiatric cases, and notes that they are always addressed through the power of the Word, which both separates and defines: 'In psychiatric cases, spiritual perceptions … are mixed with the forms of the subconscious' (*Wilt Thou Be Made Whole?*, p. 62). The 'rebuke' (*epitimao*) of Jesus separates out what has become mixed in the suffering person.
4. In a lecture he gave in St. Gallen on November 16, 1917, Rudolf Steiner said: 'Medicine can endure only if it is a spiritual science, for illnesses come from a spiritual being that only makes use of the human body in order to profit from it… Illnesses emerge because this being works in the human being.' See Rudolf Steiner, *Geographic Medicine*, p. 65.

5. As a student in the Distance Learning Program of the Seminary of the Christian Community in North America, I completed a final project based on the verses about the beam and splinter. That learning experience, along with the Open Courses and other offerings of the seminary, was crucial in shaping the ideas I have shared in this book. Interested readers can learn more at christiancommunityseminary.ca.

2. A Woman with a Fever: Mark 1:29–31
(See also Matthew 8:14–15 and Luke 4:38–39)
1. See https://womeninscripture.com/2020/10/18/peters-mother-in-law/.
2. In *The Myth of Normal*, authors Gabor and Daniel Maté quote the following from Dr Steven Cole: 'One of the things many diseases have in common is inflammation, acting as a kind of fertilizer for the development of illness. We've discovered that when people feel threatened, insecure – especially over an extended period of time – our bodies are programmed to turn on inflammatory genes.' Chapter 6, p. 94. Chronic rage raises stress hormone levels long past the period of usefulness, exacerbating anxiety and depression, suppressing immunity, and promoting vascular disease, among other pathological effects.
3. Adam Blanning, 'Inflammation as Transformation: How to Get Unstuck? Part 2', Denver Center for Anthroposophic Therapies, 2022. Available at https://www.denvertherapies.com/blog/inflammation-as-transformation-how-to-get-unstuck-part-2.

3. A Leper: Matthew 8:1–4
(See also Mark 1:40–45 and Luke 5:12–15)

4. An Invalid by the Pool of Bethesda: John 5:1–18
(See also Matthew 9:1–8, Mark 2:1–12 and Luke 5:17–26)
1. Emil Bock, *The Three Years*, p. 159.
2. The Sheep Gate was the first gate to be restored when the Temple was rebuilt as described in Nehemiah, Chapter 3. The high priest built it along with his brother priests and consecrated it, the only gate so distinguished. The pool next to this gate was used to wash sheep before their sacrifice. See: https://tncchurch.org/nehemiah-the-gospel-in-the-gates-sheep-gate-neh-3a/.

5. A Man with a Withered Hand: Mark 3:1–6
(See also Matthew 12:9–15 and Luke 6:6–11)

6. A Centurion's Servant: Luke 7:1–10
(See also Matthew 8:5–13 and John 4:46–54)
1. See https://www.bibleodyssey.org/en/places/related-articles/roman-centurion.
2. Emil Bock, *The Three Years*, pp. 175f.
3. Bastiaan Baan, *Old and New Mysteries*, p. 39.

7. The Young Man of Nain: Luke 7:11–17
1. Steiner, *Christianity as Mystical Fact*, pp. 93f.
2. Wine and Water Watch, 'We Don't Know How to Do That', May 5, 2016. http://winewaterwatch.org/2016/05/we-scientists-dont-know-how-to-do-that-what-a-commentary/.

8. A Demon-possessed Man in the Tombs: Mark 5:1–20
(See also Matthew 8:28–34 and Luke 8:26–39)
1. In his book *It Didn't Start With You*, Mark Wolynn writes: 'The first nine months outside the womb function as a continuation of the neural development that occurs within the womb. Which neural circuits remain, which are discarded, and how the remaining circuits will be organized depend on how an infant experiences and interacts with the mother or caregiver. It's through these early interactions that a child continues to establish a blueprint for managing emotions, thoughts, and behaviors … The impact of an early break in the mother-child bond … can be devastating for the infant… A separation from the mother can be felt as "life-threatening".' p. 41.
2. A method of psychotherapy called Internal Family Therapy is based on the principle that everyone has multiple 'parts' that need to be accepted, understood and loved, rather than judged, criticized and exiled. When parts are unburdened of their protective function, a self emerges that is calm, compassionate and creative. This self doesn't have to be developed, is not damaged and knows how to bring us healing. The way to achieve this is to create a healthy inner community in which each part can play its rightful role without being scapegoated or exiled. See Richard C. Schwartz, *No Bad Parts*, Sounds True, USA 2021.

3. My descriptions of Carrefour House and the people I met there are composites of different people and communities I have known. All names and identifying details have been changed.

9. A Bleeding Woman and a Dying Girl: Mark 5:21–43
(See also Matthew 9:18–26 and Luke 8:40–56)
1. Emil Bock writes: 'Rudolf Steiner drew attention repeatedly to the frequent way in which the gospels, through the very words they used, emphasize the links of destiny. The girl lacked those forces of the blood which were necessary for carrying her across the threshold of puberty. The woman, whose destiny ran parallel to the child's in such a remarkable way, suffered from a surplus of what was lacking in the other ... Healing forces radiate from Jesus in both directions, they heal the "too much" and the "too little". A golden mean reveals itself, bestowing its harmonizing power not only on individuals, but on a group of people united by destiny.' *The Three Years*, p. 179. See also Rudolf Steiner, *The Gospel of Luke*, p. 162.

10. A Gentile Woman's Daughter: Matthew 15:21–28
(See also Mark 7:24–30)
1. See Robert D. Miller, *Understanding the Old Testament Course Guidebook*, The Teaching Company, USA 2019, pp. 89–90.
2. In her interesting article 'Enemies of Israel: Ruth and the Canaanite Woman', Glenna S. Jackson compares the versions of the Canaanite woman as given in Mark and Matthew with the story of Ruth, arguing for a relationship between the rabbinic rules for conversion to Judaism (which followed the four-time request, three-time refusal pattern found in the book of Ruth) and Matthew's revision of the text. Downloaded at: https://www.researchgate.net/publication/45681463_Enemies_of_Israel_Ruth_and_the_Canaanite_Woman

11. A Deaf Man: Mark 7:31–37
(See also Matthew 9:32–34 and 12:22–32, and Luke 11:14–23)
1. See, for example, Ed Yong, *I Contain Multitudes*, Ecco, USA 2016.
2. Mark Wolynn writes: 'Traumatic memories are often stored as nondeclarative memory. When an event becomes so overwhelming that we lose our words, we cannot accurately record or 'declare' the memory

in story form, which requires language to do so. It's as though a flash flood is streaming through all our doors and windows at once. In the danger, we don't stop long enough to put our experience into words. We just leave the house.' *It Didn't Start With You*, p. 55.

3. Maya Angelou, *I Know Why the Caged Bird Sings*, Random House, USA 1969.

12. A Blind Man: Mark 8:22–26

(See also Matthew 9:27–31)

1. I must acknowledge my debt to the work of Rudolf Steiner as the basis for all these considerations, but especially this one. On the disconnected experience of percepts and the unitive world of concepts, see *The Science of Knowing* and *The Philosophy of Freedom*. On humanity's spiritual evolution and the Fall, see *An Outline of Occult Science* and *Cosmic Memory*. On the modern path of development of higher vision, see *How To Know Higher Worlds* and *A Way of Self-Knowledge*. Many other references would be possible. Anthroposophy as a whole is directed at the goal of enabling modern human beings to develop their higher faculties in a healthy, productive way, becoming 'seers' who can bring life-giving, healing impulses into our suffering world. Even if we do not yet have clairvoyant vision, when we read and understand the results of spiritual research, and confirm them with our clear, logical thinking and our healthy feeling for the truth, this becomes itself a valuable form of 'seeing'.
2. Oliver Sacks, *An Anthropologist on Mars*. See Chapter 4: To See and Not See.
3. Rudolf Frieling, *The Complete New Testament Studies*, pp. 178f.
4. Ibid.
5. *Faust: Part Two*, V.viii.4605–06.

13. A Boy with Seizures: Mark 9:14–29

(See also Matthew 17:14–20 and Luke 9:37–43)

1. Rudolf Frieling wrote a fascinating and detailed essay on the Transfiguration, which is included in the final section of *The Complete New Testament Studies*.
2. Bessel van der Kolk, *The Body Keeps the Score*, p. 204.
3. In his lecture 'How Can I Find Christ?' given on October 16, 1918, in

Zurich, Rudolf Steiner describes how the soul's experience of profound powerlessness can lead to an experience of Christ and of resurrection. See *Death as Metamorphosis of Life*.

14. A Woman with a Disabling Spirit: Luke 13:10–17

1. See *Understanding the Old Testament Course Guidebook*, Chapter 18: Daniel and Apocalyptic Literature. See also Rudolf Frieling, *The Complete Old Testament Studies*, Chapter 15: The Beasts of the Abyss and the Son of Man.

15. A Man with Dropsy: Luke 14:1–6

1. Rachel Naomi Remen, *Kitchen Table Wisdom: 10th Anniversary Edition*, Riverhead Books, USA 2006, p. 278.

16. Ten Lepers: Luke 17:11–19

1. Elsbeth Weymann, *Paths into the Book of Books*, pp. 51 and 56.
2. Bessel van der Kolk, *The Body Keeps the Score*, p. 203.

17. A Blind Man of Jericho: Mark 10:46–52

(See also Matthew 20:29–34, Luke 18:35–43 and John 9:1–41)

1. This poem was in part inspired by Elsbeth Weymann's version of Isaiah 60:1–2 in *Paths into the Book of Books* (see p. 25). I also had in mind Rudolf Steiner's beautiful verse given for eurythmy, 'He who illuminates the clouds' (*Der Wolkendurchleuchter*).
2. Oliver Sacks eloquently describes how blindness is not only an absence of sense, but another mode of being: 'Valvo quotes a patient of his as saying, "One must die as a sighted person to be born again as a blind person," and the opposite is equally true: one must die as a blind person to be born again as a seeing person. It is the interim, the limbo ... that is so terrible. Though blindness may at first be a terrible privation and loss, it may become less so with the passage of time, for a deep adaptation, or reorientation, occurs, by which one reconstitutes, reappropriates, the world in nonvisual terms. It then becomes a different condition, a different form of being, one with its own sensibilities and coherence and feeling.' *An Anthropologist on Mars*, p. 142.
3. In the lecture he gave in Munich on March 15, 1910, Steiner said: 'We

are approaching an age when people will feel they are surrounded by a physical, sensory world, but also – according to their understanding – by a spiritual kingdom. The leader in this new kingdom of the spirit will be the etheric Christ. No matter what religious community or faith people belong to, once they experience these facts within themselves, they will acknowledge and accept the Christ event.' See *The Reappearance of Christ in the Etheric*, p. 104.
4. Helen Keller, *The World I Live In*, New York Review Books, USA 2003, p. 63.

18. Lazarus: John 11:33–44
(See also Matthew 19:16–30, Mark 10:17–31 and Luke 18:18–30)
1. See Bart D. Ehrman, *Lost Christianities*, pp. 73f. See also Bastiaan Baan, *Old and New Mysteries*, p. 88.
2. Rudolf Steiner wrote and spoke often about Lazarus as the first Christian initiate. See for example *Christianity as Mystical Fact* and the lecture cycle *The Gospel of John*.
3. Weymann, *Paths into the Book of Books*, p. 13.
4. Dr Bruce D. Perry explains these principles in his books. See, for example, *What Happened To You?*, with Oprah Winfrey, Flatiron Books, USA 2021.

Afterword
1. Bessel van der Kolk, *The Body Keeps the Score*, p. 235.

Appendix 1: The Anthroposophical View of Christ and Human Evolution
1. See for example Rudolf Steiner, *The Reappearance of Christ in the Etheric*.

Bibliography

Baan, Bastiaan, *Old and New Mysteries: From Trials to Initiation*, Floris Books, UK 2014.
Bock, Emil, *The Three Years: The Life of Christ Between Baptism and Ascension*, Floris Books, UK 2005.
Brown, Brené, *Daring Greatly: How the Courage to Be Vulnerable Transforms the Way We Live, Love, Parent and Lead*, Penguin, USA 2012.
Ehrman, Bart D., *Lost Christianities: The Battles for Scripture and the Faiths We Never Knew*, Oxford University Press, UK 2005.
Frieling, Rudolf, *The Complete New Testament Studies,* Floris Books, UK 2021.
—, *The Complete Old Testament Studies*, Floris Books, UK 2021.
Kolk, Bessel van der, *The Body Keeps the Score*, Penguin, USA 2014.
Kühlewind, Georg, *Wilt Thou Be Made Whole? Healings in the Gospels*, Lindisfarne Books, UK 2008.
Lusseyran, Jacques, *And There Was Light: The Autobiography of a Blind Hero in the French Resistance*, Floris Books, UK 1985.
Maté, Gabor with Maté, Daniel, *The Myth of Normal: Trauma, Healing and Illness in a Toxic Culture*, Vermilion, UK 2022.
Rohr, Richard, *Falling Upward: A Spirituality for the Two Halves of Life*, Jossey-Bass, USA 2011.
Sacks, Oliver, *An Anthropologist on Mars*, Knopf, USA 1995.
Steiner, Rudolf, *Christianity as Mystical Fact and the Mysteries of Antiquity* (CW8), SteinerBooks, USA 2006.
—, *Death as a Metamorphosis of Life* (CW182), SteinerBooks, USA 2008.
—, *The Fifth Gospel: From the Akashic Record* (CW148), Rudolf Steiner Press, UK 2005.
—, *Geographic Medicine: Two Lectures by Rudolf Steiner*, Mercury Press, USA 2005.
—, *The Gospel of John* (CW103), SteinerBooks, USA 2022.

—, *The Gospel of Luke* (CW114), Rudolf Steiner Press, UK 1964.
—, *The Reappearance of Christ in the Etheric: A Collection of Lectures on the Second Coming of Christ*, SteinerBooks, USA 2003.
Weymann, Elsbeth, *Paths into the Book of Books: New Biblical Translations Through the Festivals of the Year*, Floris Books, UK 2015.
Wolynn, Mark, *It Didn't Start With You: How Inherited Family Trauma Shapes Who We Are and How to End the Cycle*, Viking, USA 2016.

Lory Widmer Hess is a writer, editor and caregiver, who grew up near Seattle, USA. After gaining degrees in English Literature and Education she studied anthroposophy and the arts at Sunbridge College in New York and earned a diploma in eurythmy at Eurythmy Spring Valley. She has been a member of the Christian Community since 2002.

Lory has been a book editor for the Waldorf Early Childhood Association of North America since 2006, and her own writing has been published in a variety of print and online publications. She also works part-time in a residential home for adults with developmental disabilities, and is currently training to become a spiritual director. Lory lives in Switzerland with her family and blogs at enterenchanted.com.

For news on all our **latest books**, and to receive **exclusive discounts**, **join** our mailing list at:

florisbooks.co.uk/signup

Plus subscribers get a FREE book with every online order!

We will never pass your details to anyone else.

www.ingramcontent.com/pod-product-compliance
Lightning Source LLC
Chambersburg PA
CBHW070121110526
44587CB00017BA/2858